Col

Qu

Survival

Compilers: William Allan
Ian Brooke
Elaine Henderson
Mike Munro
Ralph Neilson

HarperCollins Publishers
Westerhill Road, Bishopbriggs, Glasgow G64 2QT
www.collins.co.uk

First published 1994
This edition published 2000
Updated 2001, 2003, 2005

Reprint 10 9 8 7 6 5 4 3 2 1 0

ISBN 0 00 720349 7

Layout and design by
bounford.com
5 The Maltings, Green Drift, Royston, Herts SG8 5DY

Printed in Italy by Amadeus S.r.l.

Foreword

Have you ever tried to find the answer to what you originally thought was a relatively simple question? Have you ever searched high and low and finally given up in complete exasperation? This is the book you need, with its thousands of difficult-to-remember and hard-to-find facts. Here you will find the answers to such diverse enquiries as 'What are the member countries of NATO?' and 'Who were the Seven Fathers of the Church?' There are lists of everything from fields of study, chemical elements, winners of the Booker Prize and patron saints, to the world's five largest deserts, the seven liberal arts and the winners of the championships in all the major sports. In among the hard facts are entries on more lighthearted matters, such as the order of the presents in the song 'The Twelve Days of Christmas'.

This fascinating little book draws together material from nine distinct fields: Politics, History, Geography, Religion, Science, The Arts, Language, Sport and General Interest.

It provides an easy-to-use, quick reference point for a broad miscellany of information that could only be otherwise obtained after consulting a wide variety of sources, and as such will appeal to everyone from trivia buffs and quiz compilers to students and journalists.

Contents

Politics

Countries of the World 14
Major Political Groupings 34
Arab League 34
Andean Group (Grupo Andino) 34
APEC (Asia Pacific Economic Cooperation) 34
CARICOM (Caribbean Community and Common Market) 35
The Commonwealth 36
European Union 38
ECOWAS (Economic Community of West African States) 38
EFTA (European Free Trade Association) 39
ESA (European Space Agency) 39
NATO (North Atlantic Treaty Organization) 40
OAS (Organization of American States) 40
OAU (Organization of African Unity) 41
OECD (Organization for Economic Cooperation and Development) 42
OPEC (Organization of the Petroleum Exporting Countries) 43
United Nations 43

Administration Areas 49
Pre-1974 Counties of the United Kingdom 49
Post-1974 and post-1996 Counties/Councils/ Regions of the United Kingdom 52
Australian States/Territories and their Capitals 58
Canadian Provinces/Territories and their Capitals 58
New Zealand Regional and City Councils 59
South African Provinces and their Capitals 59
States of the United States of America 60
Nobel Peace Prize 62

History

Sovereigns of the British Isles 66
Rulers of Scotland (from 1058) 66
Principal Rulers of Wales (from 999) 67
Rulers of Ireland (from 1002) 69
Rulers of England (from 955) and of the United Kingdom (from 1801) 69
British Prime Ministers 72
US Presidents 75
Australian Prime Ministers 77
New Zealand Prime Ministers 78
Canadian Prime Ministers 79
South African Presidents 80
South African Prime Ministers 80
Roman Emperors 81
Major Battles 84
Major Wars 90

Geography

Beaufort Scale 100
Richter and Mercalli scales 102
Shipping Areas 103
Continents of the World 104
Largest Islands 104
Largest Oceans 104
Largest Seas 105
Largest Deserts 105
Highest Mountains 105
Highest Volcanoes (Active) 105
Highest Waterfalls 106
Longest Rivers 106
Largest Lakes 106
Deepest Caves 107
Largest Countries (Area) 107
Largest Countries (Population) 107
Smallest Countries (Area) 108
Smallest Countries (Population) 108
Most Densely Populated Countries with Populations over 10 million 108
Largest Cities 109
Longest Road Tunnels 109
Longest Rail Tunnels 109
Longest Bridges (Main Span) 110
Highest Dams 110

Busiest Ports 110
Busiest International Airports 111
Major Cities and their Rivers 111

Religion

The Ten Commandments 113
The Beatitudes 114
The Stations of the Cross 115
The Twelve Apostles 116
The Four Last Things 116
The Seven Sacraments 116
The Seven Champions of Christendom 117
The Seven Fathers of the Church 117
The Ten Plagues of Egypt 117
The Four Horsemen of the Apocalypse 118
The Twelve Tribes of Israel 118
The Seven Last Plagues 119
The Seven Corporal Works of Mercy 119
Saints and Saints' Days 119
Patron Saints of the British Isles 126
Patron Saints and Intercessors 126
Largest Religions 135
Types of Cross 136
Popes of the Roman Catholic Church 138
Archbishops of Canterbury 142
Books of the Bible 144
Protestant Canon 144

Roman Catholic Canon 144
Jewish Texts 147
The Koran 148
The Five Pillars of Islam 151
Sikhism 151
Hindu Texts 152
Buddhist (Pali) Texts 152
Principal Gods 153
Greek 153
Roman 154
Norse 154
Other Figures 156
Egyptian 157

Science

The Human Skeleton 158
The Seven Life Processes 158
Tissue Types 159
The Nine Organ Systems 160
Geological Table 162
Chemical Elements 164
Periodic Table 168
Mohs' Hardness Scale 170
Gemstones 170
Scientific Laws 172
Inventions 178
E numbers 184

Arts

Poets laureate 186
Man Booker Prize 187
Pulitzer Prize 189
Prix Goncourt 190
Nobel Prize in Literature 191
The Oscars 194
Musical Expression and Tempo Instructions 198

Languages

Typographic, Scientific and Mathematical Symbols 202
Accents 204
The Apostrophe 204
American Spelling and Word Variations 206
Fields of Study 208
Collective Nouns 225
Animals and Related Terms 228
Enthusiasts and Collectors 232
-Archies and -Ocracies 234
International Communication Alphabet 235
Common Acronyms 236

Sport

American Football 240
The Super Bowl 240

Association Football **241**
English Premier League Championship 241
English FA Challenge Cup 242
Scottish Premier League Championship 243
Scottish FA Challenge Cup 244
European Champion Clubs Cup 246
UEFA Cup 247
FIFA World Cup 248
European International Championship 249
Athletics **250**
The Olympic Games 250
Baseball **253**
The World Series 253
Basketball **254**
American NBA Championship 254
Cricket **256**
The County Championship 256
The Benson & Hedges Cup 257
Cheltenham & Gloucester Trophy 258
The World Cup 258
Cycling **259**
Tour de France 259
Golf **260**
The Open Championship 260
US Masters 262
US Open Championship 263

USPGA Championship 264
The Ryder Cup 265
Horse Racing **267**
The Derby Stakes 267
The Oaks Stakes 268
1,000 Guineas Stakes 269
2,000 Guineas Stakes 270
St Leger Stakes 271
The Champion Hurdle Challenge Cup 272
Cheltenham Gold Cup Steeplechase 273
Grand National Steeplechase 274
Motor Racing **276**
F1 World Drivers Championship 276
Rugby League **278**
The Challenge Cup 278
The Super League 279
The World Cup 279
Rugby Union **280**
Six Nations Championship 280
The World Cup 281
Grand Slam Winners 281
Triple Crown Winners 282
Snooker **282**
The World Professional Championship 282
Tennis **283**
Wimbledon Open Championships 283
Australian Open Championships 286

French Open Championships 287
US Open Championships 288

General Interest

International Time Zones **290**
The International Date Line **292**
Calendars **293**
Lunar Calendar 293
Solar Calendar 293
Lunisolar Calendar 294
Calendars in Use Today **294**
Gregorian Calendar 294
Jewish Calendar 296
Islamic Calendar 297
Hindu Calendar 298
Chinese Calendar 299
French Revolutionary Calendar **301**
Solstice **302**
Equinox **302**
Quarter days (England, Wales and Northern Ireland) **302**
Scottish Term Days **303**
Birthstones, Astrological Signs and Names **304**
Wedding Anniversaries **306**
Orders of Precedence **307**
Principal British Orders and Decorations in Order of Precedence **308**

Decorations for Gallantry and Distinguished Service 310
The Armed Forces 311
The Police 314
The Knights of the Round Table 315
The Four Temperaments or Humours 315
The Seven Liberal Arts 316
The Six Wives of Henry VIII 316
The Three Graces (Greek Mythology) 316
The Nine Muses (Greek Mythology) 317
The Labours of Hercules 317
The Seven Virtues 318
The Seven Wonders of the Ancient World 318
The Seven Seas 319
The Seven Deadly Sins 319
The Twelve Days of Christmas 319
The Magnificent Seven 320
The Seven Dwarfs 320
The Three Musketeers 320

Politics

COUNTRIES OF THE WORLD

Country	Area	Principal Language(s)
Afghanistan	Asia	Dari; Pushtu
Albania	Europe	Albanian
Algeria	Africa	Arabic; French
American Samoa	Oceania	Samoan; English
Andorra	Europe	Catalan; French; Spanish
Angola	Africa	Portuguese; Bantu
Anguilla (UK)	C America	English
Antigua & Barbuda	C America	English
Argentina	S America	Spanish
Armenia	Asia	Armenian
Aruba (Neth)	C America	Dutch; Papiamento; English
Australia	Oceania	English
Austria	Europe	German
Azerbaijan	Asia	Azeri
Bahamas, The	C America	English
Bahrain	Asia	Arabic; English
Bangladesh	Asia	Bengali
Barbados	C America	English
Belarus	Europe	Belarussian; Russian
Belgium	Europe	Flemish/Dutch; Walloon/French; German
Belize	C America	English; Spanish; Mayan

Currency	Capital	Population
Afghani	Kabul	23,897,000
Lek	Tirana	3,166,000
Algerian dinar	Algiers	31,800,000
US$	Fagatogo	67,000
Euro	Andorra la Vella	71,000
Kwanza	Luanda	13,625,000
E Caribbean $	The Valley	12,000
E Caribbean $	St John's	73,000
Argentinian peso	Buenos Aires	38,428,000
Dram	Yerevan	3,061,000
Aruban florin	Oranjestad	100,000
Australian $	Canberra	19,731,000
Euro	Vienna	8,116,000
Azerbaijani manat	Baku	8,370,000
Bahamian $	Nassau	314,000
Bahraini dinar	Manama	724,000
Taka	Dhaka	146,736,000
Barbados $	Bridgetown	270,000
Belarus rouble	Minsk	9,895,000
Euro	Brussels	10,318,000
Belize $	Belmopan	256,000

Country	Area	Principal Language(s)
Benin	Africa	French; Fon
Bermuda (UK)	C America	English
Bhutan	Asia	Dzongkha
Bolivia	S America	Spanish; Quechua; Aymara
Bosnia-Herzegovina	Europe	Bosnian; Serbian; Croatian
Botswana	Africa	English; Setswana
Brazil	S America	Portuguese
Brunei	Asia	Malay; English
Bulgaria	Europe	Bulgarian
Burkina	Africa	French; African languages
Burundi	Africa	French; Kirundi
Cambodia	Asia	Khmer; Vietnamese
Cameroon	Africa	French; English; African languages
Canada	N America	English; French
Cape Verde	Africa	Portuguese; Creole
Cayman Islands (UK)	C America	English
Central African Republic	Africa	French; Sango
Chad	Africa	Arabic; French; African languages
Chile	S America	Spanish
China	Asia	Mandarin; Wu; Cantonese; Hsiang
Christmas Island (Aus)	Asia	English
Cocos Islands (Aus)	Asia	English
Colombia	S America	Spanish

Currency	Capital	Population
CFA franc	Porto-Novo	6,736,000
Bermuda $	Hamilton	82,000
Ngultrum; Indian rupee	Thimphu	2,257,000
Boliviano	La Paz/Sucre	8,808,000
Marka	Sarajevo	4,161,000
Pula	Gaborone	1,785,000
Real	Brasilia	178,470,000
Brunei $	Bandar Seri Begawan	358,000
Lev	Sofia	7,897,000
CFA franc	Ouagadougou	13,002,000
Burundi franc	Bujumbura	6,825,000
Riel	Phnom Penh	14,144,000
CFA franc	Yaoundé	16,018,000
Canadian $	Ottawa	31,510,000
Cape Verde escudo	Praia	463,000
Cayman Islands $	George Town	40,000
CFA franc	Bangui	3,865,000
CFA franc	Ndjamena	8,598,000
Chilean peso	Santiago	15,805,000
Yuan; Hong Kong $; Macau pataca	Beijing	1,289,161,000
Australian $	The Settlement	1,560
Australian $	West Island	632
Colombian peso	Bogotá	44,222,000

Country	Area	Principal Language(s)
Comoros	Africa	Comorian; Arabic; French
Congo	Africa	French; African languages
Congo, Dem. Rep. of	Africa	French; African languages
Cook Islands (NZ)	Oceania	English; Maori
Costa Rica	C America	Spanish
Côte d'Ivoire	Africa	French; African languages
Croatia	Europe	Croation; Serbian
Cuba	C America	Spanish
Cyprus	Europe	Greek; Turkish; English
Czech Republic	Europe	Czech
Denmark	Europe	Danish
Djibouti	Africa	Somali; Afar; French; Arabic
Dominica	C America	English; Creole
Dominican Republic	C America	Spanish; Creole
East Timor	Asia	Portuguese; Tetun; English
Ecuador	S America	Spanish; Quechua
Egypt	Africa	Arabic
El Salvador	C America	Spanish
Equatorial Guinea	Africa	Spanish; French; Fang
Eritrea	Africa	Tigrinya; Tigre
Estonia	Europe	Estonian; Russian
Ethiopia	Africa	Oromo; Amharic; Tigrinya
Falkland Islands (UK)	S America	English
Faroe Islands	Europe	Danish; Faroese

Currency	Capital	Population
Comoros franc	Moroni	768,000
CFA franc	Brazzaville	3,724,000
Congolese franc	Kinshasa	52,771,000
New Zealand $	Auarua	18,000
Costa Rican colón	San José	4,173,000
CFA franc	Yamoussoukro	16,631,000
Kuna	Zagreb	4,428,000
Cuban peso	Havana	11,300,000
Cyprus £	Nicosia	802,000
Czech koruna	Prague	10,236,000
Danish krone	Copenhagen	5,364,000
Djibouti franc	Djibouti	703,000
E Caribbean $	Roseau	79,000
Dominican peso	Santo Domingo	8,745,000
US $	Dili	778,000
US $	Quito	13,003,000
Egyptian £	Cairo	71,931,000
El Salvador colón; US $	San Salvador	6,515,000
CFA franc	Malabo	494,000
Nakfa	Asmara	4,141,000
Kroon	Tallinn	1,323,000
Birr	Addis Ababa	70,678,000
Falkland Islands £	Stanley	3,000
Danish krone	Thorshavn	47,000

Country	Area	Principal Language(s)
Fiji	Oceania	English; Fijian; Hindi
Finland	Europe	Finnish; Swedish
France	Europe	French
French Guiana	S America	French; Creole
French Polynesia	Oceania	French; Tahitian
Gabon	Africa	French; Fang
Gambia, The	Africa	English; African languages
Georgia	Asia	Georgian; Russian
Germany	Europe	German
Ghana	Africa	English; African languages
Gibraltar (UK)	Europe	English; Spanish
Greece	Europe	Greek
Greenland (Den)	N America	Danish; Greenlandic
Grenada	C America	English; Creole
Guadeloupe (Fr)	C America	French; Creole
Guam (US)	Oceania	English; Chamorro; Tagalog
Guatemala	C America	Spanish; Mayan languages
Guernsey (UK)	Europe	English; French
Guinea	Africa	French; African languages
Guinea-Bissau	Africa	Portuguese; Crioulo; African languages
Guyana	S America	English; Creole; Amerindian languages
Haiti	C America	French; Creole
Honduras	C America	Spanish; Amerindian languages
Hungary	Europe	Hungarian

Currency	Capital	Population
Fiji $	Suva	839,000
Euro	Helsinki	5,207,000
Euro	Paris	60,144,000
Euro	Cayenne	178,000
CFP franc	Papeete	244,000
CFA franc	Libreville	1,329,000
Dalasi	Banjul	1,426,000
Lari	T'bilisi	5,126,000
Euro	Berlin	82,476,000
Cedi	Accra	20,922,000
Gibraltar £	Gibraltar	27,000
Euro	Athens	10,976,000
Danish krone	Nuuk	57,000
E Caribbean $	St George's	80,000
Euro	Basse-Terre	440,000
US $	Hagåtña	163,000
Quetzal; US $	Guatemala City	12,347,000
£ sterling	St Peter Port	62,701
Guinea franc	Conakry	8,480,000
CFA franc	Bissau	1,493,000
Guyana $	Georgetown	765,000
Gourde	Port-au-Prince	8,326,000
Lempira	Tegucigalpa	6,941,000
Forint	Budapest	9,877,000

Country	Area	Principal Language(s)
Iceland	Europe	Icelandic
India	Asia	Hindi; English; Indian languages
Indonesia	Asia	Indonesian; local languages
Iran	Asia	Farsi
Iraq	Asia	Arabic; Kurdish
Ireland, Republic of	Europe	English; Irish
Isle of Man (UK)	Europe	English
Israel	Asia	Hebrew; Arabic
Italy	Europe	Italian
Jamaica	C America	English; Creole
Japan	Asia	Japanese
Jersey (UK)	Europe	English; French
Jordan	Asia	Arabic
Kazakhstan	Asia	Kazakh; Russian
Kenya	Africa	English; Swahili; African languages
Kiribati	Oceania	English; Gilbertese
Korea, North	Asia	Korean
Korea, South	Asia	Korean
Kuwait	Asia	Arabic
Kyrgyzstan	Asia	Kyrgyz; Russian
Laos	Asia	Lao
Latvia	Europe	Latvian; Russian
Lebanon	Asia	Arabic; Armenian; French
Lesotho	Africa	Sesotho; English; Zulu

** De facto capital. Disputed.*

Currency	Capital	Population
Icelandic króna	Reykjavik	290,000
Indian rupee	New Delhi	1,065,462
Rupiah	Jakarta	219,883,000
Iranian rial	Tehrān	68,920,000
Iraqi dinar	Baghdad	25,175,000
Euro	Dublin	3,956,000
£ sterling	Douglas	75,000
Shekel	*Jerusalem	6,433,000
Euro	Rome	57,423,000
Jamaican $	Kingston	2,651,000
Yen	Tokyo	127,654,000
£ sterling	St Helier	87,186
Jordanian dinar	'Ammān	5,473,000
Tenge	Astana	15,433,000
Kenyan shilling	Nairobi	31,987,000
Australian $	Bairiki	88,000
North Korean won	P'yŏngyang	22,664,000
South Korean won	Seoul	47,700,000
Kuwaiti dinar	Kuwait	2,521,000
Kyrgyz som	Bishkek	5,138,000
Kip	Vientiane	5,657,000
Lats	Riga	2,307,000
Lebanese £	Beirut	3,653,000
Loti; South African rand	Maseru	1,802,000

Country	Area	Principal Language(s)
Liberia	Africa	English; Creole; African languages
Libya	Africa	Arabic; Berber
Liechtenstein	Europe	German
Lithuania	Europe	Lithuanian; Russian
Luxembourg	Europe	French; German; Letzeburgish
Macedonia	Europe	Macedonian
Madagascar	Africa	Malagasy; French
Malawi	Africa	English; Chichewa
Malaysia	Asia	Malay; English; Chinese; Tamil
Maldives	Asia	Divehi
Mali	Africa	French; African languages
Malta	Europe	Maltese; English
Mariana Islands, Northern (US)	Oceania	English; Chamorro
Marshall Islands	Oceania	Marshallese; English
Martinique (Fr)	C America	French; Creole
Mauritania	Africa	Arabic; French
Mauritius	Africa	English; French; Hindi; Creole
Mexico	N America	Spanish; Amerindian languages
Micronesia, Fed States of	Oceania	English; indigenous languages
Moldova	Europe	Romanian; Ukrainian; Gagauz; Russian
Monaco	Europe	French; Monégasque
Mongolia	Asia	Khalkha
Montserrat (UK)	C America	English

Currency	Capital	Population
Liberian $	Monrovia	3,367,000
Libyan dinar	Tripoli	5,551,000
Swiss franc	Vaduz	34,000
Litas	Vilnius	3,444,000
Euro	Luxembourg	453,000
Macedonian denar	Skopje	2,056,000
Malagasy franc	Antananarivo	17,404,000
Malawian kwacha	Lilongwe	12,105,000
Ringgit	Kuala Lumpur/Putrajaya	24,425,000
Rufiyaa	Male	318,000
CFA franc	Bamako	13,007,000
Maltese lira	Valletta	394,000
US $	Capitol Hill	79,000
US $	Delap-Uliga-Djarrit	53,000
Euro	Fort-de-France	393,000
Ouguiya	Nouakchott	2,893,000
Mauritius rupee	Port Louis	1,221,000
Mexican peso	Mexico City	103,457,000
US $	Palikir	109,000
Moldovan leu	Chişinău	4,267,000
Euro	Monaco-Ville	34,000
Tugrik	Ulan Bator	2,594,000
E Caribbean $	Plymouth	4,000

Country	Area	Principal Language(s)
Morocco	Africa	Arabic; French; Berber
Mozambique	Africa	Portuguese; African languages
Myanmar (Burma)	Asia	Burmese
Namibia	Africa	English; Afrikaans; German
Nauru	Oceania	Nauruan; English
Nepal	Asia	Nepali
Netherlands	Europe	Dutch; Frisian
Netherlands Antilles (Neth)	C America	Dutch; Papiamento; English
New Caledonia (Fr)	Oceania	French; Melanesian languages
New Zealand	Oceania	English; Maori
Nicaragua	C America	Spanish; Amerindian languages
Niger	Africa	French; Hausa
Nigeria	Africa	English; Hausa; Yoruba
Niue	Oceania	English; Polynesian
Norway	Europe	Norwegian
Oman	Asia	Arabic; Baluchi; Indian languages
Pakistan	Asia	Urdu; Punjabi; English
Palau	Oceania	Palauan; English
Panama	C America	Spanish; English
Papua New Guinea	Oceania	English; Tok Pisin (Creole)
Paraguay	S America	Spanish; Guarani
Peru	S America	Spanish; Quechua; Aymara
Philippines	Asia	Filipino; English; Tagalog
Pitcairn Islands	Oceania	English

Currency	Capital	Population
Moroccan dirham	Rabat	30,566,000
Metical	Maputo	18,863,000
Kyat	Rangoon	49,485,000
Namibian $	Windhoek	1,987,000
Australian $	Yaren	13,000
Nepalese rupee	Kathmandu	25,164,000
Euro	Amsterdam/The Hague	16,149,000
Netherlands Antilles guilder	Willemstad	221,000
CFP franc	Nouméa	228,000
New Zealand $	Wellington	3,875,000
Córdoba	Managua	5,466,000
CFA franc	Niamey	11,972,000
Naira	Abuja	124,009,000
NZ $	Alofi	2,000
Norwegian krone	Oslo	4,533,000
Omani riyal	Muscat	2,851,000
Pakistani rupee	Islamabad	153,578,000
US $	Koror	20,000
Balboa	Panama City	3,120,000
Kina	Port Moresby	5,711,000
Guarani	Asunción	5,878,000
Sol	Lima	27,167,000
Philippine peso	Manila	79,999,000
New Zealand $	Adamstown	51

Country	Area	Principal Language(s)
Poland	Europe	Polish
Portugal	Europe	Portuguese
Puerto Rico (US)	C America	Spanish; English
Qatar	Asia	Arabic
Réunion (Fr)	Africa	French; Creole
Romania	Europe	Romanian
Russian Federation	Europe/Asia	Russian; Tatar; Ukrainian
Rwanda	Africa	French; Kinyarwanda; English
St Helena & Dependencies (UK)	Africa	English
St Kitts & Nevis	C America	English; Creole
St Lucia	C America	English; Creole
St Pierre & Miquelon (Fr)	N America	French
St Vincent & the Grenadines	C America	English; Creole
Samoa	Oceania	Samoan; English
San Marino	Europe	Italian
São Tomé & Príncipe	Africa	Portuguese; Creole
Saudi Arabia	Asia	Arabic
Senegal	Africa	French; Wolof
Serbia & Montenegro	Europe	Serbian; Albanian; Hungarian
Seychelles	Africa	Creole; French; English
Sierra Leone	Africa	English; African languages

Currency	Capital	Population
Zloty	Warsaw	38,587,000
Euro	Lisbon	10,062,000
US $	San Juan	3,879,000
Qatar riyal	Doha	610,000
Euro	St-Denis	756,000
Romanian leu	Bucharest	22,334,000
Russian rouble	Moscow	143,246,000
Rwandan franc	Kigali	8,387,000
St Helena £; £ sterling	Jamestown	7,050
E Caribbean $	Basseterre	42,000
E Caribbean $	Castries	149,000
Euro	St-Pierre	6,000
E Caribbean $	Kingstown	120,000
Tala	Apia	178,000
Euro	San Marino	28,000
Dobra	São Tomé	161,000
Saudi Arabian riyal	Riyadh	24,217,000
CFA franc	Dakar	10,095,000
Serbian dinar; Euro	Belgrade	10,527,000
Seychelles rupee	Victoria	81,000
Leone	Freetown	4,971,000

Country	Area	Principal Language(s)
Singapore	Asia	English; Malay; Chinese; Tamil
Slovakia	Europe	Slovakian; Hungarian; Czech
Slovenia	Europe	Slovenian; Croatian; Serbian
Solomon Islands	Oceania	English; indigenous languages
Somalia	Africa	Somali; Arabic
South Africa	Africa	Afrikaans; English; African languages
Spain	Europe	Spanish; Catalan; Galician; Basque
Sri Lanka	Asia	Sinhalese; Tamil; English
Sudan	Africa	Arabic; African languages
Suriname	S America	Dutch; Surinamese
Swaziland	Africa	English; Swazi
Sweden	Europe	Swedish
Switzerland	Europe	German; French; Italian; Romansch
Syria	Asia	Arabic; Kurdish
Taiwan	Asia	Mandarin; indigenous languages
Tajikistan	Asia	Tajik; Uzbek; Russian
Tanzania	Africa	Swahili; English
Thailand	Asia	Thai; Lao; Chinese
Togo	Africa	French; African languages
Tonga	Oceania	Tongan; English
Trinidad & Tobago	C America	English; Creole
Tunisia	Africa	Arabic; French
Turkey	Asia	Turkish; Kurdish
Turkmenistan	Asia	Turkmen; Russian; Uzbek

Currency	Capital	Population
Singapore $	Singapore	4,253,000
Slovakian koruna	Bratislava	5,402,000
Tolar	Ljubljana	1,984,000
Solomon Islands $	Honiara	477,000
Somali shilling	Mogadishu	9,890,000
Rand	Pretoria/Cape Town	45,026,000
Euro	Madrid	41,060,000
Sri Lankan rupee	Sri Jayewardenepura Kotte	19,065,000
Sudanese dinar	Khartoum	33,610,000
Suriname guilder	Paramaribo	436,000
Emalangeni; South African rand	Mbabane	1,077,000
Swedish krona	Stockholm	8,876,000
Swiss franc	Bern	7,169,000
Syrian £	Damascus	17,800,000
Taiwan $	T'aipei	22,548,000
Somoni	Dushanbe	6,245,000
Tanzanian shilling	Dodoma	36,977,000
Baht	Bangkok	62,833,000
CFA franc	Lomé	4,909,000
Pa'anga	Nuku'alofa	104,000
Trinidad & Tobago $	Port of Spain	1,303,000
Tunisian dinar	Tunis	9,832,000
Turkish lira	Ankara	71,325,000
Turkmen manat	Ashgabat	4,867,000

Country	Area	Principal Language(s)
Turks & Caicos Islands (UK)	C America	English
Tuvalu	Oceania	Tuvaluan; English
Uganda	Africa	English; Swahili; African languages
Ukraine	Europe	Ukrainian; Russian
United Arab Emirates	Asia	Arabic; English
United Kingdom*	Europe	English; Welsh; Gaelic
United States of America	N America	English; Spanish
Uruguay	S America	Spanish
Uzbekistan	Asia	Uzbek; Russian
Vanuatu	Oceania	Bislama; English; French
Vatican City	Europe	Italian
Venezuela	S America	Spanish; Amerindian languages
Vietnam	Asia	Vietnamese; Thai; Khmer; Chinese
Virgin Islands (UK)	C America	English
Virgin Islands (US)	C America	English; Spanish
Wallis & Futuna Islands (Fr)	Oceania	French; indigenous languages
Yemen	Asia	Arabic
Zambia	Africa	English; African languages
Zimbabwe	Africa	English; African languages
**England*	–	–
Northern Ireland	–	–
Scotland	–	–
Wales	–	–

Currency	Capital	Population
US $	Grand Turk	21,000
Australian $	Vaiaku	11,000
Ugandan shilling	Kampala	25,827,000
Hyrvnia	Kiev	48,523,000
UAE dirham	Abu Dhabi	2,995,000
£ sterling	London	58,789,000
US $	Washington DC	294,043,000
Uruguayan peso	Montevideo	3,415,000
Uzbek som	Tashkent	26,093,000
Vatu	Port Vila	212,000
Euro	Vatican City	472,000
Bolivar	Caracas	25,699,000
Dong	Ha Nôi	81,377,000
US $	Road Town	21,000
US $	Charlotte Amalie	111,000
CFP franc	Matā'utu	15,000
Yemeni riyal	Şan'ā'	20,010,000
Zambian kwacha	Lusaka	10,812,000
Zimbabwean $	Harare	12,891,000
–	*London*	*49,138,831*
–	*Belfast*	*1,685,267*
–	*Edinburgh*	*5,062,011*
–	*Cardiff*	*2,903,085*

MAJOR POLITICAL GROUPINGS

Arab League

Founded in 1945 to promote Arab unity. Original members shown in italics.

Members			
Algeria	*Jordan*	Oman	*Syria*
Bahrain	Kuwait	Palestine	Tunisia
Comoros	*Lebanon*	Qatar	UAE
Djibouti	Libya	*Saudi Arabia*	*Yemen*
Egypt	Mauritania	Somalia	
Iraq	Morocco	Sudan	

Andean Group (Grupo Andino)

South American organization founded in 1969 for economic and social cooperation between members. Original members shown in italics.

Members				
Bolivia	*Colombia*	*Ecuador*	*Peru*	Venezuela

Chile withdrew in 1977.

APEC (Asia Pacific Economic Cooperation)

Initiated in November 1989 as an informal consultative forum to promote multilateral economic cooperation on issues of trade and development. Original members shown in italics.

Members

Australia	*Malaysia*	Russia (1998)
Brunei	*Mexico*	*South Korea*
Canada	*New Zealand*	*Singapore*
Chile	*Papua New Guinea*	*Taiwan**
China	Peru (1998)	*Thailand*
Indonesia	*Philippines*	*USA*
Japan		Vietnam (1998)

** Admitted as Chinese Taipei.*

CARICOM (Caribbean Community and Common Market)

Established in 1973 by the Treaty of Chaguaramas for foreign policy and economic and social coordination in the Caribbean region.

Members

Antigua & Barbuda	Jamaica
Bahamas, The	Montserrat
Barbados*	St Kitts & Nevis
Belize	St Lucia
Dominica	St Vincent & the Grenadines
Grenada	Suriname
Guyana	Trinidad & Tobago
Haiti	

** Barbados is a member of the Community but not of the Common Market.*

Associate members

Anguilla
Bermuda
British Virgin Islands
Cayman Islands
Turks & Caicos Islands

Observer status

Aruba
Colombia
Dominican Republic
Mexico
Netherlands Antilles
Puerto Rico
Venezuela

The Commonwealth

An informal association of sovereign states, without charter or constitution but coordinated by the Commonwealth Secretariat in London. Inaugurated in 1926 and based originally on membership of the British Empire. It is now a multi-racial association of equal, independent nations.

Members (and date of joining)

Antigua & Barbuda (1981)
Australia (1931)
Bahamas, The (1973)
Bangladesh (1972)
Barbados (1966)
Belize (1981)
Botswana (1966)
Brunei (1984)
Cameroon (1995)
Canada (1931)
Cyprus (1961)
Dominica (1978)
Fiji (1970; membership lapsed 1987; rejoined 1997)
Gambia, The (1965)
Ghana (1957)
Grenada (1974)
Guyana (1966)

Members (and date of joining) *cont.*

India (1947)
Jamaica (1962)
Kenya (1963)
Kiribati (1979)
Lesotho (1966)
Malawi (1964)
Malaysia (1957)
Maldives (1982)
Malta (1964)
Mauritius (1968)
Mozambique (1995)
Namibia (1990)
Nauru (1968)
New Zealand (1931)Nigeria (1960)
Pakistan (1947; left 1972; rejoined 1989)
Papua New Guinea (1975)
St Kitts & Nevis (1983)
St Lucia (1979)
St Vincent & the Grenadines (1979)
Samoa (1970)
Seychelles (1976)
Sierra Leone (1961)
Singapore (1965)
Solomon Islands (1978)
South Africa (1931; left 1961; rejoined 1994)
Sri Lanka (1948)
Swaziland (1968)
Tanzania (1961)
Tonga (1970)
Trinidad & Tobago (1962)
Tuvalu (1978)
Uganda (1962)
United Kingdom (1931)
Vanuatu (1980)
Zambia (1964)
Zimbabwe (1980; suspended March 2002)

Countries which have left the Commonwealth: Republic of Ireland (1949).

European Union

Founded in 1957 as the European Economic Community to establish a Common Market.

Later became the EC (European Community) and in 1993 the EU (European Union). Original members shown in italics.

Members

Austria (1995)*	Latvia (2004)
*Belgium**	Lithuania (2004)
Cyprus (2004)	*Luxembourg**
Czech Republic (2004)	Malta (2004)
Denmark (1973)	*Netherlands**
Estonia (2004)	Poland (2004)
Finland (1995)*	Portugal (1986)*
*France**	Slovakia (2004)
*Germany**	Slovenia (2004)
Greece (1981)	Spain (1986)*
Hungary (2004)	Sweden (1995)
Ireland, Republic of (1973)*	United Kingdom (1973)
*Italy**	

** Founder members of the European single currency (1999).*

ECOWAS (Economic Community of West African States)

Founded in 1975 for the promotion of economic cooperation and development by the Treaty of Lagos.

Members

Benin	Ghana	Niger
Burkina	Guinea	Nigeria
Cape Verde	Guinea-Bissau	Senegal
Côte d'Ivoire	Liberia	Sierra Leone
Gambia, The	Mali	Togo

EFTA (European Free Trade Association)

Established in 1960.

Members*

Iceland Liechtenstein Norway Switzerland

** Founding members Austria, Denmark, Finland, Portugal, Sweden and UK left to join the EU.*

ESA (European Space Agency)

Founded in 1975. Engages its members in space research and technology.

Members

Austria	Greece	Portugal
Belgium	Ireland, Rep. of	Spain
Denmark	Italy	Sweden
Finland	Luxembourg	Switzerland
France	Netherlands	United Kingdom
Germany	Norway	

Canada and Hungary are cooperating states.

NATO (North Atlantic Treaty Organization)

Founded in 1949. Original members shown in italics.

Belgium	Hungary (1999)	*Portugal*
Bulgaria (2004)	*Iceland*	Romania (2004)
Canada	*Italy*	Slovakia (2004)
Czech Republic (1999)	Latvia (2004)	Slovenia (2004)
Denmark	Lithuania (2004)	Spain (1982)
France	*Luxembourg*	Turkey (1952)
Germany*	*Netherlands*	*United Kingdom*
Greece (1952)	*Norway*	*United States of America*
	Poland (1999)	

**The Federal Republic of Germany was admitted in 1955 and reunited Germany in 1990.*

OAS (Organization of American States)

Founded in 1948 to promote peace, security and the economic development of the western hemisphere. Original members shown in italics.

Members

Antigua & Barbuda (1981)	Canada (1990)	*Ecuador*
Argentina	*Chile*	*El Salvador*
Bahamas, The (1982)	*Colombia*	Grenada (1975)
Barbados (1967)	*Costa Rica*	*Guatemala*
Belize (1991)	*Cuba (suspended 1962)*	Guyana (1991)
Bolivia	Dominica (1979)	*Haiti*
Brazil	*Dominican Republic*	*Honduras*
		Jamaica (1969)
		Mexico

Original members *cont.*

Nicaragua
Panama
Paraguay
Peru
St Kitts & Nevis (1984)
St Lucia (1979)
St Vincent & the Grenadines (1981)
Suriname (1977)
Trinidad & Tobago (1967)
United States of America
Uruguay
Venezuela

OAU (Organization of African Unity)

Established in 1963 to eradicate colonialism and improve economic, cultural and political cooperation in Africa.

Members

Algeria
Angola
Benin
Botswana
Burkina
Burundi
Cameroon
Cape Verde
Central African Republic
Chad
Comoros
Congo, Rep. of
Congo, Dem. Rep. of
Côte d'Ivoire
Djibouti
Egypt
Equatorial Guinea
Eritrea
Ethiopia
Gabon
Gambia, The
Ghana
Guinea
Guinea-Bissau
Kenya
Lesotho
Liberia
Libya
Madagascar
Malawi
Mali
Mauritania
Mauritius
Mozambique
Namibia
Niger
Nigeria
Rwanda
São Tomé & Príncipe
Senegal
Seychelles
Sierra Leone

Members *cont.*

Somalia
South Africa
Sudan
Swaziland
Tanzania
Togo
Tunisia
Uganda
Zambia
Zimbabwe

OECD (Organization for Economic Cooperation and Development)

Founded in 1961 to promote the economic growth of the member countries, to coordinate and improve development aid and to expand world trade. Original members shown in italics.

Members

Australia (1971)
Austria
Belgium
Canada
Czech Republic (1995)
Denmark
Finland (1969)
France
Germany
Greece
Hungary (1996)
Iceland
Ireland, Republic of
Italy (1962)
Japan (1964)
South Korea (1996)
Luxembourg
Mexico (1994)
Netherlands
New Zealand (1973)
Norway
Poland (1996)
Portugal
Slovakia (2000)
Spain
Sweden
Switzerland
Turkey
United Kingdom
United States of America

OPEC (Organization of the Petroleum Exporting Countries)

Established in 1960 to coordinate price and supply policies of oil-producing states.

Members*

Algeria	Kuwait	Saudi Arabia
Indonesia	Libya	United Arab Emirates
Iran	Nigeria	Venezuela
Iraq	Qatar	

** Ecuador withdrew in 1992 and Gabon in 1995.*

United Nations

Founded in 1945.

The six main organs are:

General Assembly	Assembly of all members.
Security Council	15 members – 5 permanent (China, France, Russia, UK, US), 10 non-permanent members elected for a 2-year period.
Economic and Social Council	54 non-permanent members elected for a 3-year period.

The six main organs are *cont.*	
Trusteeship Council	China, France, Russia, UK, US.
International Court of Justice	Main judicial organ of the UN. Consists of 15 judges, each from a different member state chosen by the General Assembly and the Security Council for a 9-year term. Sits at The Hague.
Secretariat	Secretary-General and a large international staff. Secretary-General is the chief administration officer and serves a 5-year term.

Specialized agencies of the UN and their affiliation dates:

FAO	Food and Agriculture Organization (1945)
IAEA	International Atomic Energy Agency (1957)
IBRD	International Bank for Reconstruction and Development (1945)
ICAO	International Civil Aviation Organization (1947)
IDA	International Development Association (1960)
IFC	International Finance Corporation (1956)
IFAD	International Fund for Agricultural Development (1977)
ILO	International Labour Organization (1946)
IMO	International Maritime Organization (1948)
IMF	International Monetary Fund (1945)
ITU	International Telecommunications Union (1947)
UNESCO	United Nations Education Scientific and Cultural Organization (1946)

Specialized agencies *cont.*

UPU	Universal Postal Union (1947)
WHO	World Health Organization (1948)
WIPO	World Intellectual Property Organization (1974)
WMO	World Meteorological Organization (1950)
WTO	World Trade Organization (1995)

Other agencies

UNHCR	UN High Commission for Refugees
UNICEF	UN International Children's Emergency Fund
UNIDO	UN Industrial Development Organization
UNRRA	UN Relief and Rehabilitation Administration
IUCN	International Union for the Conservation of Nature and Natural Resources

Members (and date of joining; founder members in italic)

Afghanistan	1946	Bahrain	1971
Albania	1955	Bangladesh	1974
Algeria	1962	Barbados	1966
Andorra	1993	*Belarus*	1945
Angola	1976	*Belgium*	1945
Antigua & Barbuda	1981	Belize	1981
Argentina	1945	Benin	1960
Armenia	1992	Bhutan	1971
Australia	1945	*Bolivia*	1945
Austria	1955	Bosnia-Herzegovina	1992
Azerbaijan	1992	Botswana	1966
Bahamas, The	1973	*Brazil*	1945

Members (and date of joining; founder members in italic) *cont.*

Brunei	1984	*Ecuador*	1945
Bulgaria	1955	*Egypt*	1945
Burkina	1960	*El Salvador*	1945
Burundi	1962	Equatorial Guinea	1968
Cambodia	1955	Eritrea	1993
Cameroon	1960	Estonia	1991
Canada	1945	*Ethiopia*	1945
Cape Verde	1975	Fed. States of Micronesia	1991
Central African Rep.	1960	Fiji	1970
Chad	1960	Finland	1955
Chile	1945	*France*	1945
*China**	1945	Gabon	1960
Colombia	1945	Gambia, The	1965
Comoros	1975	Georgia	1992
Congo, Rep. of	1960	Germany***	1973
Congo, Dem. Rep. of **	1960	Ghana	1957
Costa Rica	1945	*Greece*	1945
Côte d'Ivoire	1960	Grenada	1974
Croatia	1992	*Guatemala*	1945
Cuba	1945	Guinea	1958
Cyprus	1960	Guinea-Bissau	1974
Czechoslovakia	1945–93	Guyana	1966
Czech Republic	1993	*Haiti*	1945
Denmark	1945	*Honduras*	1945
Djibouti	1977	Hungary	1955
Dominica	1978	Iceland	1946
Dominican Republic	1945	*India*	1945

** Taiwan to 1971 ** Formerly Zaire *** Originally admitted as separate Federal Republic of Germany and German Democratic Republic. Germany from 1990.*

Members (and date of joining; founder members in italic) *cont.*

Indonesia	1950	Mali	1960
Iran	1945	Malta	1964
Iraq	1945	Marshall Islands	1991
Ireland, Rep. of	1955	Mauritania	1961
Israel	1949	Mauritius	1968
Italy	1955	*Mexico*	1945
Jamaica	1962	Moldova	1992
Japan	1956	Monaco	1991
Jordan	1955	Mongolia	1961
Kazakhstan	1992	Morocco	1956
Kenya	1963	Mozambique	1975
Korea, North	1991	Myanmar (Burma)	1948
Korea, South	1991	Namibia	1990
Kuwait	1963	Nepal	1955
Kyrgyzstan	1992	*Netherlands*	1945
Laos	1955	*New Zealand*	1945
Latvia	1991	*Nicaragua*	1945
Lebanon	1945	Niger	1960
Lesotho	1966	Nigeria	1960
Liberia	1945	*Norway*	1945
Libya	1955	Oman	1971
Liechtenstein	1990	Pakistan	1947
Lithuania	1991	Palau	1994
Luxembourg	1945	*Panama*	1945
Macedonia	1993	Papua New Guinea	1975
Madagascar	1960	*Paraguay*	1945
Malawi	1964	*Peru*	1945
Malaysia	1957	*Philippines*	1945
Maldives	1965	*Poland*	1945

Members (and date of joining; founder members in italic) *cont.*

Portugal	1955	Switzerland	2002
Qatar	1971	*Syria*	1945
Romania	1955	Tajikistan	1992
Russian Federation	1991	Tanzania	1961
Rwanda	1962	Thailand	1946
St Kitts & Nevis	1983	Togo	1960
St Lucia	1979	Trinidad & Tobago	1962
St Vincent & the Grenadines	1980	Tunisia	1956
		Turkey	1945
San Marino	1992	Turkmenistan	1992
São Tomé & Príncipe	1975	Uganda	1962
Saudi Arabia	1945	*Ukraine*	1945
Senegal	1960	United Arab Emirates	1971
Serbia & Montenegro	2000	*United Kingdom*	1945
Seychelles	1976	*United States of America*	1945
Sierra Leone	1961	*Uruguay*	1945
Singapore	1965	USSR	1945–91
Slovakia	1993	Uzbekistan	1992
Slovenia	1992	Vanuatu	1981
Solomon Islands	1978	*Venezuela*	1945
Somalia	1960	Vietnam	1977
South Africa	1945	Western Samoa	1976
Spain	1955	Yemen Arab Rep. (N)	1947–90
Sri Lanka	1955	Yemen PDR (S)	1967–90
Sudan	1956	Yemen	1990
Suriname	1975	*Yugoslavia*	1945–92*
Swaziland	1968	Zambia	1964
Sweden	1946	Zimbabwe	1980

* *Yugoslavia was suspended in 1992*

ADMINISTRATION AREAS

Pre-1974 Counties of the United Kingdom

England

County	Abbreviation	County Town
Bedfordshire	Beds	Bedford
Berkshire	Berks	Reading
Buckinghamshire	Bucks	Aylesbury
Cambridgeshire	Cambs	Cambridge
Cheshire	Ches	Chester
Cornwall	Corn	Bodmin
Cumberland	Cumb	Carlisle
Derbyshire	Derby	Derby
Devon		Exeter
Dorset		Dorchester
Durham	Dur	Durham
Essex		Chelmsford
Gloucestershire	Glos	Gloucester
Hampshire	Hants	Winchester
Herefordshire		Hereford
Hertfordshire	Herts	Hertford
Huntingdonshire	Hunts	Huntingdon
Kent		Maidstone
Lancashire	Lancs	Lancaster
Leicestershire	Leics	Leicester
Lincolnshire	Lincs	Lincoln
Middlesex	Middx	Brentford
Norfolk		Norwich
Northamptonshire	Northants	Northampton

England *cont.*

County	Abbreviation	County Town
Northumberland	Northumb	Newcastle upon Tyne
Nottinghamshire	Notts	Nottingham
Oxfordshire	Oxon	Oxford
Rutland		Oakham
Shropshire	Salop	Shrewsbury
Somerset	Som	Taunton
Staffordshire	Staffs	Stafford
Suffolk		Ipswich
Surrey		Kingston upon Thames
Sussex		Lewes
Warwickshire	War	Warwick
Westmorland		Appleby
Wiltshire	Wilts	Salisbury
Worcestershire	Worcs	Worcester
Yorkshire	Yorks	York

Scotland

County	County Town
Aberdeenshire	Aberdeen
Angus	Forfar
Argyllshire & Islands	Inveraray
Ayrshire	Ayr
Banffshire	Banff
Berwickshire	Duns
Buteshire & Isle of Arran	Rothesay
Caithness	Wick
Clackmannanshire	Alloa
Dunbartonshire	Dumbarton

Scotland *cont.*

County	**County Town**
Dumfriesshire	Dumfries
East Lothian	Haddington
Fife	Cupar
Inverness-shire	Kinross
Kirkcudbrightshire	Kirkcudbright
Lanarkshire	Lanark
Midlothian	Edinburgh
Morayshire	Elgin
Nairnshire	Nairn
Orkney Islands	Kirkwall
Peeblesshire	Peebles
Perthshire	Perth
Renfrewshire	Renfrew
Ross & Cromarty and Isle of Lewis	Dingwall
Roxburghshire	Jedburgh
Selkirkshire	Selkirk
Shetland Islands	Lerwick
Stirlingshire	Stirling
Sutherland	Dornoch
West Lothian	Linlithgow
Wigtownshire	Wigtown

Wales

County	**County Town**
Anglesey	Beaumaris
Brecknockshire	Brecon
Caernarvonshire	Caernarvon

Wales *cont.*

County	County Town
Cardiganshire	Cardigan
Carmarthenshire	Carmarthen
Denbighshire	Ruthin
Flintshire	Mold
Glamorgan	Cardiff
Merionethshire	Dolgelley
Monmouthshire	Monmouth
Montgomeryshire	Welshpool
Pembrokeshire	Haverfordwest
Radnorshire	Presteigne

Northern Ireland

County	County Town
Antrim	Belfast
Armagh	Armagh
Down	Downpatrick
Fermanagh	Enniskillen
Londonderry	Londonderry
Tyrone	Omagh

Post-1974 and post-1996 Counties/Councils/Regions of the United Kingdom

England (1974–96) Counties

Avon
Bedfordshire
Berkshire
Buckinghamshire
Cambridgeshire
Cheshire
Cleveland
Cornwall/Isles of Scilly
Cumbria
Derbyshire
Devon

England (1974–96) Counties *cont.*

Dorset
Durham
East Sussex
Essex
Gloucestershire
Greater London
Greater Manchester
Hampshire
Hereford & Worcester
Hertfordshire
Humberside
Isle of Wight
Kent
Lancashire
Leicestershire
Lincolnshire
Merseyside
Norfolk
Northamptonshire
Northumberland
North Yorkshire
Nottinghamshire
Oxfordshire
Shropshire
Somerset
South Yorkshire
Staffordshire
Suffolk
Surrey
Tyne & Wear
Warwickshire
West Midlands
West Sussex
West Yorkshire
Wiltshire

English (post-1996) County Councils

Bedfordshire
Buckinghamshire
Cambridgeshire
Cheshire
Cornwall
Cumbria
Derbyshire
Devon
Dorset
Durham
East Sussex
Essex
Gloucestershire
Hampshire
Hertfordshire
Kent
Lancashire
Leicestershire
Lincolnshire
Norfolk
Northampton
North Yorkshire
Northumberland
Nottinghamshire
Oxfordshire
Shropshire
Somerset
Staffordshire
Suffolk
Surrey
Warwickshire
West Sussex
Wiltshire
Worcestershire

English (post-1996) Unitary Councils

Bath & Northeast Somerset	Kingston upon Hull	Slough
Blackburn with Darwen	Leicester	Southend on Sea
Blackpool	Luton	South Gloucestershire
Bournemouth	Medway	Southampton
Bracknell Forest	Middlesbrough	Stockton-on-Tees
Brighton and Hove	Milton Keynes	Stoke-on-Trent
Bristol	Northeast Lincolnshire	Swindon
Darlington	North Lincolnshire	Telford & Wrekin
Derby	North Somerset	Thurrock
East Riding of Yorkshire	Nottingham	Torbay
Halton	Peterborough	Warrington
Hartlepool	Plymouth	West Berkshire
Herefordshire	Poole	Windsor & Maidenhead
Isle of Wight	Portsmouth	Wokingham
Isles of Scilly	Reading	York
	Redcar & Cleveland	
	Rutland	

English (post-1996) Metropolitan Councils

Barnsley	Gateshead	Oldham
Birmingham	Kirklees	Rochdale
Bolton	Knowsley	Rotherham
Bradford	Leeds	St Helens
Bury	Liverpool	Salford
Calderdale	Manchester	Sandwell
Coventry	Newcastle upon Tyne	Sefton
Doncaster	North Tyneside	Sheffield
Dudley		Solihull

English (post-1996) Metropolitan Councils *cont.*

South Tyneside
Stockport
Sunderland
Tameside
Trafford
Wakefield
Walsall
Wigan
Wirral
Wolverhampton

Greater London Borough Councils

Greater London Authority
Corporation of London
Barking & Dagenham
Barnet
Bexley
Brent
Bromley
Camden
Croydon
Ealing
Enfield
Greenwich
Hackney
Hammersmith & Fulham
Haringey
Harrow
Havering
Hillingdon
Hounslow
Islington
Kensington & Chelsea
Kingston upon Thames
Lambeth
Lewisham
Merton
Newham
Redbridge
Richmond upon Thames
Southwark
Sutton
Tower Hamlets
Waltham Forest
Wandsworth
Westminster

Scotland

Regions (1975–96)	**Unitary Councils (post-1996)**
Borders	Scottish Borders
Central	Clackmannanshire, Falkirk, Stirling
Dumfries & Galloway	Dumfries & Galloway
Fife	Fife
Grampian	Aberdeen City, Aberdeenshire, Moray

Scotland *cont.*	
Highland	Highland
Lothian	East Lothian, City of Edinburgh, Midlothian, West Lothian
Tayside	Angus, Dundee City, Perth & Kinross
Strathclyde	Argyll & Bute, East Ayrshire, North Ayrshire, South Ayrshire, West Dunbartonshire, East Dunbartonshire, Glasgow City, Inverclyde, North Lanarkshire, South Lanarkshire, East Renfrewshire, Renfrewshire
Orkney Islands	Orkney Islands
Shetland Islands	Shetland Islands
Western Isles	Western Isles

Wales (1974–96) Counties

Clwyd	Gwynedd	South Glamorgan
Dyfed	Mid Glamorgan	West Glamorgan
Gwent	Powys	

Unitary Councils (post-1996)

Anglesey	Denbighshire	Powys
Blaenau Gwent	Flintshire	Rhondda Cynon Taff
Bridgend	Gwynedd	Swansea
Caerphilly	Merthyr Tydfil	Torfaen
Cardiff	Monmouthshire	Vale of Glamorgan
Carmarthenshire	Neath & Port Talbot	Wrexham
Ceredigion	Newport	
Conwy	Pembrokeshire	

Northern Ireland District Councils (post-1996)

Antrim	Coleraine	Limavady
Ards	Cookstown	Lisburn
Armagh	Craigavon	Magherafelt
Ballymena	Derry	Moyle
Ballymoney	Down	Newtownabbey
Banbridge	Dungannon & South Tyrone	Newry & Mourne
Belfast	Fermanagh	North Down
Carrickfergus	Larne	Omagh
Castlereagh		Strabane

Republic of Ireland Provinces/Counties

Province	**County**	**County Town**
Connacht	Galway	Galway
	Leitrim	Carrick-on-Shannon
	Mayo	Castlebar
	Roscommon	Roscommon
	Sligo	Sligo
Leinster	Carlow	Carlow
	Dublin	Dublin
	Kildare	Naas
	Kilkenny	Kilkenny
	Laoighis	Portlaoise
	Longford	Longford
	Louth	Dundalk
	Meath	Trim
	Offaly	Tullamore
	Westmeath	Mullingar
	Wexford	Wexford
	Wicklow	Wicklow

Republic of Ireland Provinces/Counties *cont.*

Munster	Clare	Ennis
	Cork	Cork
	Kerry	Tralee
	Limerick	Limerick
	Tipperary	Clonmel
	Waterford	Waterford
Ulster	Cavan	Cavan
	Donegal	Lifford
	Monaghan	Monaghan

Australian States/Territories and their Capitals

Australian Capital Territory	Canberra
New South Wales	Sydney
Northern Territory	Darwin
Queensland	Brisbane
South Australia	Adelaide
Tasmania	Hobart
Victoria	Melbourne
Western Australia	Perth

Canadian Provinces/Territories and their Capitals

Alberta	Edmonton
British Columbia	Victoria
Manitoba	Winnipeg
New Brunswick	Fredericton
Newfoundland	St John's
Northwest Territories	Yellowknife
Nova Scotia	Halifax
Ontario	Toronto

Prince Edward Island	Charlottetown
Quebec	Quebec
Saskatchewan	Regina
Yukon Territory	Whitehorse

New Zealand Regional and City Councils

Regional Councils

Auckland	Manawatu-Wanganui	Southland	West Coast
Bay of Plenty	Northland	Taranaki	
Canterbury	Otago	Waikato	
Hawke's Bay		Wellington	

City Councils

Auckland	Hutt	Nelson	Porirua
Christchurch	Invercargill	North Shore	Upper Hutt
Dunedin	Manukau	Palmerston North	Waitakere
Hamilton	Napier		Wellington

South African Provinces and their Capitals

Eastern Cape	Bisho
Free State	Bloemfontein
Gauteng	Johannesburg/Pretoria
KwaZulu Natal	Pietermaritzburg/Ulundi
Mpumalanga	Nelspruit
Northern Cape	Kimberley
Northern Transvaal	Pietersburg
North-West	Mmabatho
Western Cape	Cape Town

States of the United States of America

State	Capital	Abbrev	Postal Abbrev	Nickname
Alabama	Montgomery	Ala	AL	Yellowhammer State
Alaska	Juneau	Alas	AK	Last Frontier
Arizona	Phoenix	Ariz	AZ	Grand Canyon State
Arkansas	Little Rock	Ark	AR	The Natural State
California	Sacramento	Calif	CA	Golden State
Colorado	Denver	Colo	CO	Centennial State
Connecticut	Hartford	Conn	CT	Constitution State
Delaware	Dover	Del	DE	Diamond State
Florida	Tallahassee	Fla	FL	Sunshine State
Georgia	Atlanta	Ga	GA	Peach State
Hawaii	Honolulu		HI	Aloha State
Idaho	Boise		ID	Gem State
Illinois	Springfield	Ill	IL	Land of Lincoln
Indiana	Indianapolis	Ind	IN	Hoosier State
Iowa	Des Moines	Ia	IA	Hawkeye State
Kansas	Topeka	Kan	KS	Sunflower State
Kentucky	Frankfort	Ky	KY	Bluegrass State
Louisiana	Baton Rouge	La	LA	Pelican State
Maine	Augusta	Me	ME	Pine Tree State
Maryland	Annapolis	Md	MD	Old Line State
Massachusetts	Boston	Mass	MA	Bay State
Michigan	Lansing	Mich	MI	Great Lakes State
Minnesota	St Paul	Minn	MN	North Star State
Mississippi	Jackson	Miss	MS	Magnolia State
Missouri	Jefferson City	Mo	MO	Show Me State

State	Capital	Abbrev	Postal Abbrev	Nickname
Montana	Helena	Mont	MT	Treasure State
Nebraska	Lincoln	Nebr	NB	Cornhusker State
Nevada	Carson City	Nev	NV	The Silver State
New Hampshire	Concord		NH	Granite State
New Jersey	Trenton		NJ	Garden State
New Mexico	Santa Fe	NMex	NM	Land of Enchantment
New York	Albany		NY	Empire State
North Carolina	Raleigh		NC	Tar Heel State
North Dakota	Bismarck	NDak	ND	Peace Garden State
Ohio	Columbus		OH	Buckeye State
Oklahoma	Oklahoma City	Okla	OK	Sooner State
Oregon	Salem	Oreg	OR	Beaver State
Pennsylvania	Harrisburg	Pa	PA	Keystone State
Rhode Island	Providence		RI	The Ocean State
South Carolina	Columbia		SC	Palmetto State
South Dakota	Pierre	SDak	SD	Mount Rushmore State
Tennessee	Nashville	Tenn	TN	Volunteer State
Texas	Austin	Tex	TX	Lone Star State
Utah	Salt Lake City		UT	Beehive State
Vermont	Montpelier	Vt	VT	Green Mountain State
Virginia	Richmond	Va	VA	The Old Dominion State
Washington	Olympia	Wash	WA	Evergreen State
West Virginia	Charleston	WVa	WV	Mountain State
Wisconsin	Madison	Wis	WI	Badger State
Wyoming	Cheyenne	Wyo	WY	Equality State/Cowboy State

NOBEL PEACE PRIZE

1901	Jean Henri Dunant; Frédéric Passy
1902	Elie Ducommun; Charles Albert Gobat
1903	Sir William Randall Cremer
1904	Institute of International Law
1905	Baroness Bertha Sophie Felicita von Suttner
1906	Theodore Roosevelt
1907	Ernesto Moneta; Louis Renault
1908	Klas Arnoldson; Fredrik Bajer
1909	August Beernaert; Baron de Constant de Rebeque d'Estournelles
1910	International Peace Bureau
1911	Tobias Asser; Alfred Fried
1912	Elihu Root
1913	Henri La Fontaine
1914	*No award*
1915	*No award*
1916	*No award*
1917	International Red Cross Committee
1918	*No award*
1919	Thomas Woodrow Wilson
1920	Léon Bourgeois
1921	Karl Branting; Christian Lange
1922	Fridtjof Nansen
1923	*No award*
1924	*No award*
1925	Sir Austen Chamberlain; Charles Dawes
1926	Aristide Briand; Gustav Stresemann
1927	Ferdinand Buisson; Ludwig Quidde

1928 *No award*
1929 Frank B Kellogg
1930 Nathan Söderblom
1931 Jane Addams; Nicholas Butler
1932 *No award*
1933 Sir Norman Angell
1934 Arthur Henderson
1935 Carl von Ossietzky
1936 Carlos Saavedra Lamas
1937 Viscount Cecil of Chelwood
1938 Nansen International Office for Refugees
1939 *No award*
1940 *No award*
1941 *No award*
1942 *No award*
1943 *No award*
1944 International Red Cross Committee
1945 Cordell Hull
1946 Emily Balch; John R Mott
1947 American Friends Service Committee
1948 *No award*
1949 Baron Boyd Orr of Brechin Mearns
1950 Ralph Bunche
1951 Léon Jouhaux
1952 Albert Schweitzer
1953 George C Marshall
1954 Office of the United Nations High Commissioner for Refugees
1955 *No award*

1956	*No award*
1957	Lester B Pearson
1958	Georges Pire
1959	Philip Noel-Baker
1960	Albert Lutuli
1961	Dag Hammarskjöld
1962	Linus Pauling
1963	International Red Cross Committee; League of Red Cross Societies
1964	Martin Luther King, Jr
1965	UNICEF (United Nations Children's Fund)
1966	*No award*
1967	*No award*
1968	René Cassin
1969	International Labour Organization
1970	Norman Borlaug
1971	Willy Brandt
1972	*No award*
1973	Henry Kissinger; Le Duc Tho (declined)
1974	Seán MacBride; Eisaku Sato
1975	Andrei Sakharov
1976	Mairead Corrigan; Betty Williams
1977	Amnesty International
1978	Menachem Begin; Anwar al-Sadat
1979	Mother Teresa
1980	Adolfo Pérez Esquivel
1981	Office of the United Nations High Commissioner for Refugees
1982	Alfonso García Robles; Alva Myrdal

1983	Lech Walesa
1984	Desmond Tutu
1985	International Physicians for the Prevention of Nuclear War
1986	Elie Wiesel
1987	Oscar Arias Sánchez
1988	United Nations Peacekeeping Forces
1989	The Dalai Lama
1990	Mikhail Gorbachev
1991	Aung San Suu Kyi
1992	Rigoberta Menchú Tum
1993	Nelson Mandela; FW de Klerk
1994	Yasser Arafat; Shimon Peres; Yitzhak Rabin
1995	Joseph Rotblat; the Pugwash Conferences on Science and World Affairs
1996	Carlos Filipe Ximenes Belo; José Ramos-Horta
1997	Jody Williams; International Campaign to Ban Landmines
1998	John Hume; David Trimble
1999	Médecins Sans Frontières
2000	Kim Dae Jung
2001	United Nations; Kofi Annan
2002	Jimmy Carter
2003	Shirin Ebadi
2004	Wangari Maathai

History

SOVEREIGNS OF THE BRITISH ISLES

Rulers of Scotland (from 1058)

House of Dunkeld	
Malcolm III (Canmore)	1058–93
Donald Ban	1093–4
Duncan II	1094
Donald Ban (*restored*)	1094–7
Edgar	1097–07
Alexander I (the Fierce)	1107–24
David I (the Saint)	1124–53
Malcolm IV (the Maiden)	1153–65
William I (the Lion)	1165–1214
Alexander II	1214–49
Alexander III	1249–86
Margaret, Maid of Norway	1286–1290
John Balliol	1292–6
Robert I (the Bruce)	1306–29
David II	1329–71
House of Stuart	
Robert II	1371–90
Robert III	1390–1406
James I	1406–37
James II	1437–60
James III	1460–88
James IV	1488–1513
James V	1513–42
Mary, Queen of Scots	1542–67
James VI (*ascended the throne of England 1603*)	1567–1625

Principal Rulers of Wales (from 999)

Deheubarth (Seisyllwg, Brycheiniog and Dyfed)	
Llywelyn ap Seisyll	1018–23
Rhydderch ap Iestyn (usurper)	1023
Maredudd ap Edwin	1033–35
Hywel ap Edwin	1033, 1042–4
Gruffyd ap Llywelyn (King of Gwynedd & Powys from 1039)	
Gruffyd ap Llywelyn (second time)	1055–63
Maredudd ab Owain ab Edwin	c.1064
Rhys ap Owain	1072
Rhys ap Tewdwr	1078
Gruffydd ap Rhys	1135
Anarawd ap Gruffydd	1137–43
Cadell ap Gruffydd	1137–c.1151
Maredudd ap Gruffydd	c.1151–55
Rhys ap Gruffydd	c.1151–97
Gwynedd	
Cynan ap Hywel	999
Llywelyn ap Seisyll	1005
Iago ap Idwal ap Meurig	1023–39
Gwynedd & Powys annexed by Gruffydd ap Llywelyn, King of Deheubarth	1039
Bleddyn ap Cynfyn ap Gwerstan	1063
Trahaearn ap Caradog (twice)	1075
Gruffydd ap Cynan ap Iago	1075, 1081, c.1094
Owain Gwynedd	1137–70
Gwynedd divided between Cadwaladr ap Gruffydd and his sons	1170–1200

Morgannwg (Glywysing and Gwent)	
Rhys ap Owain ap Morgan	?
Hywel ap Owain ap Morgan	?
Meurig ap Hywel seized Gwent	c.1040
Cadwgan ap Meurig	c.1040–c.1055
Morgannwg taken by Llywelyn ap Iorwerth, King of Gwynedd	1055
Cadwgan ap Meurig (second time)	1063
Caradog ap Gruffydd ap Rhydderch	
Iestyn ap Gwrgant (usurper) dispossessed by King William	c.1073
Rufus of England	1081–c.1093
Powys	
Held by Gruffydd ap Llywelyn, of Deheubarth	1039–63
Bleddyn ap Cynfyn ap Gwerstan/Rhiwallon ap Cynfyn (d. 1070)	1063
Madog ap Bleddyn/Rhirid ap Bleddyn	1075–88
Cadwgan ap Bleddyn	1075–1109
Madog ap Rhirid/Ithel ap Rhirid	1109–10
Territory frequently divided	1110–1200

By 1200 Welsh kings were lords owing allegiance to England and by 1282 Edward I had conquered Wales. His son was the first English Prince of Wales (b. Caernarfon, 25 April 1284).

Rulers of Ireland (from 1002)*

Máelsechnaill mac Domnaill	(d. 1022)
Brian Bóruma mac Cennétig	(d. 1014)
Tairrdelbach Ua Briain	(d. 1086)
Muirchertach Ua Briain	(d. 1119)
Domnall Ua Lochlainn	(d. 1121)
Tairrdelbach Ua Conchobair	(d. 1156)
Muirchertach mac Lochlainn	(d. 1166)
Ruaidrí Ua Conchobair	(d. 1198)**

** The most powerful kings of the pre-Norman period.*
*** The last native King of Ireland. The Pope granted Ireland to King Henry II of England in 1172. Viking power in Ireland ended at the Battle of Clontarf in 1014. The 150 years of fighting which followed for the High Kingship contributed largely to the end of Irish royal rule.*

Rulers of England (from 955) and of the United Kingdom (from 1801)

Saxon Line	
Edwy	955–9
Edgar	959–75
Edward the Martyr	975–8
Ethelred the Unready	978–1016
Edmund Ironside	1016
Danish Line	
Canute (Cnut)	1016–35
Harold I	1035–40
Hardicanute (Harthacnut)	1040–2

Saxon Line	
Edward the Confessor	1042–66
Harold II (Godwinson)	1066
House of Normandy	
William I (The Conqueror)	1066–87
William II	1087–1100
Henry I	1100–35
Stephen	1135–54
House of Plantagenet	
Henry II (Curtmantel)	1154–89
Richard I (The Lionheart)	1189–99
John (Lackland)	1199–1216
Henry III	1216–72
Edward I (Hammer of the Scots)	1272–1307
Edward II	1307–27
Edward III	1327–77
Richard II	1377–99
House of Lancaster	
Henry IV	1399–1413
Henry V	1413–22
Henry VI	1422–61
House of York	
Edward IV	1461–83
Edward V	1483
Richard III (Crookback)	1483–5

House of Tudor	
Henry VII	1485–1509
Henry VIII	1509–47
Edward VI	1547–53
Jane (The Nine Days' Queen)	1553
Mary I (Bloody Mary)	1553–8
Elizabeth I (The Virgin Queen)	1558–1603
House of Stuart	
James I of England and VI of Scotland	1603–25
Charles I	1625–49
Commonwealth (declared 1649)	
Oliver Cromwell, Lord Protector	1653–8
Richard Cromwell	1658–9
House of Stuart	
Charles II	1660–85
James II of England and VII of Scotland	1685–8
William III and Mary II (Mary d. 1694)	1689–1702
Anne	1702–14
House of Hanover	
George I	1714–27
George II	1727–60
George III (Farmer George)	1760–1820
George IV	1820–30
William IV (Silly Billy)	1830–7
Victoria	1837–1901

House of Saxe-Coburg-Gotha	
Edward VII	1901–10
House of Windsor*	
George V (The Sailor King)	1910–36
Edward VIII (Our Smiling Prince)	1936
George VI	1936–52
Elizabeth II	1952–

** George V, originally of the House of Saxe-Coburg-Gotha, decreed on 17 July 1917 that in future it would be known as the House of Windsor, because of anti-German feeling in the First World War.*

BRITISH PRIME MINISTERS

Monarch	Prime Minister	Party	Term of Office
George II	Sir Robert Walpole	Whig	1721–42
	Earl of Wilmington	Whig	1742–3
	Henry Pelham	Whig	1743–54
	Duke of Newcastle	Whig	1754–6
	Duke of Devonshire	Whig	1756–7
	Duke of Newcastle	Whig	1757–60
George III	Duke of Newcastle	Whig	1760–2
	Earl of Bute	Tory	1762–3
	George Grenville	Whig	1763–5
	Marquis of Rockingham	Whig	1766
	Earl of Chatham	Tory	1766–8
	Duke of Grafton	Whig	1768–9
	Lord North	Tory	1770–82
	Marquis of Rockingham	Whig	1782
	Earl of Shelburne	Whig	1782–3

Monarch	Prime Minister	Party	Term of Office
	Duke of Portland	Coalition	1783
	William Pitt	Tory	1783–1801
	Viscount Sidmouth	Tory	1801–4
	William Pitt	Tory	1804–6
	Lord Grenville	Whig	1806–7
	Duke of Portland	Tory	1807–9
	Spencer Perceval	Tory	1809–12
George IV	Earl of Liverpool	Tory	1812–27
	George Canning	Tory	1827
	Viscount Goderich	Tory	1827
	Duke of Wellington	Tory	1827–30
William IV	Earl Grey	Whig	1830–4
	Viscount Melbourne	Whig	1834
	Sir Robert Peel	Tory	1834–5
	Viscount Melbourne	Whig	1835–7
Victoria	Viscount Melbourne	Whig	1837–41
	Sir Robert Peel	Tory	1841–6
	Lord John Russell	Whig	1846–52
	Earl of Derby	Tory	1852
	Earl of Aberdeen	Peelite	1852–5
	Viscount Palmerston	Liberal	1855–8
	Earl of Derby	Tory	1858–9
	Viscount Palmerston	Liberal	1859–65
	Lord John Russell	Liberal	1865–6
	Earl of Derby	Conservative	1866–8
	Benjamin Disraeli	Conservative	1868
	W E Gladstone	Liberal	1868–74
	Benjamin Disraeli	Conservative	1874–80
	W E Gladstone	Liberal	1880–5
	Marquis of Salisbury	Conservative	1885–6
	W E Gladstone	Liberal	1886
	Marquis of Salisbury	Conservative	1886–92

Monarch	Prime Minister	Party	Term of Office
	W E Gladstone	Liberal	1892–4
	Earl of Rosebery	Liberal	1894–5
	Marquis of Salisbury	Conservative	1895–1901
Edward VII	Marquis of Salisbury	Conservative	1901–2
	A J Balfour	Conservative	1902–5
	Sir H Campbell-Bannerman	Llberal	1905–8
	H H Asquith	Liberal	1908–10
George V	H H Asquith	Liberal	1910–15
	H H Asquith	Coalition	1915–16
	D Lloyd George	Coalition	1916–22
	A Bonar Law	Conservative	1922–3
	S Baldwin	Conservative	1923–4
	J R Macdonald	Labour	1924
	S Baldwin	Conservative	1924–9
	J R Macdonald	Labour	1929–31
	J R Macdonald	National	1931–5
	S Baldwin	National	1935–6
Edward VIII (abdicated 1936)			
George VI	S Baldwin	National	1936–7
	A N Chamberlain	National	1937–9
	A N Chamberlain	War Cabinet	1939–40
	W S Churchill	War Cabinet	1940–5
	W S Churchill	Caretaker	1945
	C R Attlee	Labour	1945–51
	Sir W S Churchill	Conservative	1951–2
Elizabeth II	Sir W S Churchill	Conservative	1952–5
	Sir A Eden	Conservative	1955–7
	H Macmillan	Conservative	1957–63
	Sir A Douglas-Home	Conservative	1963–4
	H Wilson	Labour	1964–70

Monarch	Prime Minister	Party	Term of Office
	E Heath	Conservative	1970–4
	H Wilson	Labour	1974–6
	J Callaghan	Labour	1976–9
	M Thatcher	Conservative	1979–90
	J Major	Conservative	1990–7
	T Blair	Labour	1997–

US PRESIDENTS

President	Party	Term of Office
George Washington	Fed	1789–97
John Adams	Fed	1797–1801
Thomas Jefferson	Rep	1801–9
James Madison	Rep	1809–17
James Monroe	Rep	1817–25
John Quincy Adams	Rep	1825–9
Andrew Jackson	Dem	1829–37
Martin van Buren	Dem	1837–41
William H Harrison	Whig	1841
John Tyler	Whig	1841–5
James K Polk	Dem	1845–9
Zachary Taylor	Whig	1849–50
Millard Fillmore	Whig	1850–3
Franklin Pierce	Dem	1853–7
James Buchanan	Dem	1857–61
Abraham Lincoln	Rep	1861–5
Andrew Johnson	Rep	1865–9

President	Party	Term of Office
Ulysses S Grant	Rep	1869–77
Rutherford B Hayes	Rep	1877–81
James A Garfield	Rep	1881
Chester A Arthur	Rep	1881–5
Grover Cleveland	Dem	1885–9
Benjamin Harrison	Rep	1889–93
Grover Cleveland	Dem	1893–7
William McKinley	Rep	1897–1901
Theodore Roosevelt	Rep	1901–9
William Howard Taft	Rep	1909–13
Woodrow Wilson	Dem	1913–21
Warren G Harding	Rep	1921–3
Calvin Coolidge	Rep	1923–9
Herbert C Hoover	Rep	1929–33
Franklin D Roosevelt	Dem	1933–45
Harry S Truman	Dem	1945–53
Dwight D Eisenhower	Rep	1953–61
John F Kennedy	Dem	1961–3
Lyndon B Johnson	Dem	1963–9
Richard M Nixon	Rep	1969–74
Gerald R Ford	Rep	1974–7
James Carter	Dem	1977–81
Ronald Reagan	Rep	1981–9
George Bush	Rep	1989–93
William Jefferson Clinton	Dem	1993–2001
George W Bush	Rep	2001–

AUSTRALIAN PRIME MINISTERS

Name	Appointed
Edmund Barton	1901
Alfred Deakin	1903; 1905; 1909
J C Watson	1904
George Reid	1904
Andrew Fisher	1908; 1914
Joseph Cook	1913
W Hughes	1915
S M Bruce	1923
J H Scullin	1929
J A Lyons	1932
Sir Earle Page	1939
R W G Menzies	1939; 1949
A W Fadden	1941
John Curtin	1941
F M Forde	1945
J B Chifley	1945
Harold Edward Holt	1966
John G Gorton	1968
William McMahon	1971
E G Whitlam	1972
Malcolm Fraser	1975
R J L Hawke	1983
Paul Keating	1991
John Howard	1996

NEW ZEALAND PRIME MINISTERS

Name	Appointed
William Hall-Jones	1906
Sir Joseph George Ward	1906; 1928
Thomas MacKenzie	1912
William Ferguson Massey	1912; 1919
Sir Francis Henry Dillon Bell	1925
Joseph Gordon Coates	1925
George William Forbes	1930; 1931
Michael Joseph Savage	1935
Peter Fraser	1940
Sidney George Holland	1949
Sir Keith Jacka Holyoake	1957; 1960
Walter Nash	1957
John Ross Marshall (later Sir)	1972
Norman Eric Kirk	1973
Wallace Edward Rowling	1974
Sir Robert David Muldoon	1975
David Russell Lange	1984
Geoffrey Winston Russell Palmer	1989
J B Bolger	1990
Jenny Shipley	1997
Helen Clark	1999

CANADIAN PRIME MINISTERS

Name	Appointed
John Alexander MacDonald	1867;1878
Alexander Mackenzie	1873
John J C Abbot	1891
John S D Thompson	1892
Mackenzie Bowell	1894
Charles Tupper	1896
Wilfrid Laurier	1896
Robert Laird Borden	1911
Arthur Meighen	1920;1926
William Lyon Mackenzie King	1921;1926;1935
Richard Bedford Bennett	1930
Louis Stephen St Laurent	1948
John George Diefenbaker	1957
Lester Bowles Pearson	1963
Pierre Elliot Trudeau	1968;1980
Joseph Clark	1979
John Napier Turner	1984
M Brian Mulroney	1984
Kim Campbell	1993
Jean Chrétien	1993
Paul Martin	2003

SOUTH AFRICAN PRESIDENTS

Name	Appointed
Charles Robberts Swart	1961
Theophilus Ebenhaezer Dönges	1967
Jozua François Nandé	1967
Jacobus Johannes Fouché	1968
Nicolaas Diederichs	1975
Balthazar Johannes Vorster	1978
Marais Viljoen	1979
Pieter Willem Botha	1984
Frederick Willem de Klerk	1989
Nelson Rolihlahla Mandela	1994
Thabo Mbeki	1999

SOUTH AFRICAN PRIME MINISTERS

Name	Appointed
Louis Botha	1910
Jan Christiaan Smuts	1919
James Barry Munnick Hertzog	1924
Jan Christiaan Smuts	1939
Daniel François Malan	1948
Johannes Gerardus Strijdom	1954
Hendrik Frensch Verwoerd	1958
Balthazar Johannes Vorster	1966
Pieter Willem Botha*	1978

**Since the resignation of PW Botha in 1989 there have been no further prime ministers.*

ROMAN EMPERORS

Where dates overlap, this indicates a period of joint rule.

Name	Dates of reign
Augustus	27 BC–AD 14
Tiberius	14–37
Caligula	37–41
Claudius	41–54
Nero	54–68
Galba	68–69
Otho	69
Vitellius	69
Vespasian	69–79
Titus	79–81
Domitian	81–96
Nerva	96–98
Trajan	98–117
Hadrian	117–138
Antoninus Pius	138–161
Marcus Aurelius	161–180
Lucius Verus (jointly with Marcus Aurelius)	161–169
Commodus	176–192
Pertinax	193
Didius Julianus	193
Septimius Severus	193–211
Caracalla	198–217
Geta	209–212
Macrinus	217–218

Name	Dates of reign
Elagabalus	218–222
Alexander Severus	222–235
Maximin	235–238
Gordian I	238
Gordian II	238
Maximus	238
Balbinus	238
Gordian III	238–244
Philip	244–249
Decius	249–251
Hostilian	251
Gallus	251–253
Aemilian	253
Valerian	253–260
Gallienus	253–268
Claudius II	268–269
Quintillus	269–270
Aurelian	270–275
Tacitus	275–276
Florian	276
Probus	276–282
Carus	282–283
Carinus	283–285
Numerian	283–284
Diocletian (east)*	284–305
Maximian (west)	286–305
Galerius (east)	305–311
Constantius I	305–306
Severus (west)	306–307

Name	Dates of reign
Maxentius (west)	306–312
Constantine I	306–337
Licinius (east)	308–324
Constantine II	337–340
Constans I	337–350
Constantius II	337–361
Magnentius	350–351
Julian	360–363
Valentinian I (west)	364–375
Valens (east)	364–378
Procopius (east)	365–366
Gratian (west)	375–383
Valentinian II (west)	375–392
Theodosius I	379–395
Arcadius (east)	395–408
Honorius (west)	395–423
Theodosius II (east)	408–450
Constantius III (west)	421–423
Valentinian III (west)	423–455
Marcian (east)	450–457
Petronius Maximus (west)	455
Avitus (west)	455–456
Leo I (east)	457–474
Majorian (west)	457–461
Libius Severus (west)	461–467
Anthemius (west)	467–472
Olybrius (west)	472–473
Julius Nepos (west)	474–480
Leo II (east)	474

Name	Dates of reign
Zeno (east)	474–491
Romulus Augustus (west)	475–476

**Diocletian initiated (AD 293) the practice of having two emperors, one ruling in the west and the other in the east. In 395 the Empire was*

MAJOR BATTLES

Name	Date
Aboukir Bay (or The Nile)	1798
Actium	31 BC
Agincourt	1415
Alamo	1836
Austerlitz	1805
Balaclava	1856
Bannockburn	1314
Bay of Pigs	1961
Blenheim	1704
Bosworth Field	1485
Boyne	1690
Britain	1940
Bulge, The	1944
Bull Run (Manassas; 1st)	1861

divided by Theodosius into the Western Roman Empire, which lasted until the sack of Rome in 476, and the Eastern Roman Empire, whose capital was Byzantium (or Constantinople, now Istanbul) and which lasted until it fell to the Turks in 1453.

Combatants	**Victor**
Royal Navy (Nelson) v. French fleet	Nelson
Octavian v. Antony and Cleopatra	Octavian
English v. French	English
Texan insurgents v. Mexican government	Mexican government
France v. Austria and Russia	France
Russia v. Britain and France	Britain and France
English (Edward II) v. Scots (Robert the Bruce)	Scots
Cubans v. US-backed anti-Castro Cuban exiles	Cubans
England and Austria v. France	England and Austria
Yorkists v. Lancastrians	Yorkists
James II v. William III	William III
Royal Air Force v. Luftwaffe	Royal Air Force
Allies v. Germany	Allies
Confederacy v. Union	Confederacy

Name	Date
Bull Run (Manassas; 2nd)	1862
Bunker Hill	1775
Crécy	1346
Culloden	1746
D-Day (Allied invasion of Europe)	1944
Dien Bien Phu	1954
Easter Rising	1916
Ebro	1938
El Alamein	1942
Flodden	1513
Gettysburg	1864
Hastings	1066
Isandhlwana	1879
Jutland	1916
Killiekrankie	1689
Lepanto	1571
Little Bighorn (Custer's Last Stand)	1876
Marathon	490 BC
Marne	1914
Marston Moor	1644
Midway	1942
Mons Graupius	AD 84
Otterburn	1388

Combatants	Victor
Confederacy v. Union	Confederacy
American Revolutionaries v. British	British
French v. English	English
Jacobites v. British government	British government
Allies v. Germany	Allies
French v. Vietnamese	Vietnamese
Irish Nationalists v. British government	British government
Spanish Nationalists v. Republican government	Nationalists
British v. Germans	British
English v. Scots	English
Union v. Confederacy	Union
English v. Normans	Normans
Zulus v. British	Zulus
Royal Navy v. German fleet	inconclusive
Jacobites v. British government	Jacobites
Spanish and Italian fleet v. Turks	Spain and Italy
Sioux and Cheyenne v. US Cavalry	Sioux and Cheyenne
Athens v. Persians	Athens
French and British v. Germans	French and British
Parliamentarians v. Royalists	Parliamentarians
US Navy v. Japanese Navy (mainly fought by carrier-based aircraft)	US Navy
Scots (Calgacus) v. Romans (Agricola)	Agricola
English v. Scots	Scots

Name	Date
Passchendaele	1917
Pearl Harbor	1941
Pharsalus	45 BC
Prestonpans	1745
Quebec	1759
Rorke's Drift	1879
Singapore	1942
Solferino	1859
Somme	1916
Spanish Armada	1588
St Albans	1455
Stalingrad	1942–3
Tannenberg	1914
Tel el-Kebir	1882
Trafalgar	1805
Valmy	1792
Verdun	1916
Waterloo	1815
Yorktown	1781

Combatants	Victor
British v. Germans	inconclusive
USA v. Japanese air attack	Japanese
Julius Caesar v. Pompey	Julius Caesar
Jacobites v. British government	Jacobites
British v. French	British
Zulus v. British	British
British v. Japanese	Japanese
French v. Austrians	French
British v. Germans	inconclusive
English v. Spanish fleet	England
Yorkists v. Lancastrians	Yorkists
Russians v. Germans	Russians
Germans v. Russians	Germans
British v. Egyptians	British
Royal Navy (Nelson) v. French and Spanish fleet	Nelson
France v. Prussians	France
French v. Germans	French
British and Prussians v. France	British and Prussians
American Revolutionaries v. British	American Revolutionaries

MAJOR WARS

Name	Dates
American Civil War	1861–65
American War of Independence	1775–83
Boer War (1st)	1880–81
Boer War (2nd)	1899–1902
Boxer Rising	1898–1900
Chinese Civil War	1946–49
Crimean War	1853–56
Crusade (1st)	1096–99
Crusade (2nd)	1147–48
Crusade (3rd)	1189–92
Dutch Wars of Independence	1568–1648
English Civil War	1642–46

Combatants	Outcome
Union v. Confederacy	Union defeats secessionist Confederacy; slavery abolished
American colonists v. British	Americans win independence from Britain
Boers v. British	Boers defeat British attempt to conquer them
Boers v. British	British defeat Boers and protect their interests in South Africa
Chinese rebels against foreign encroachments	Rising suppressed; foreign interests in China consolidated
Communists v. Nationalists	Victorious Communists establish People's Republic
Russia v. Britain, France, Turkey and Sardinia	Russia forced to give up conquered territory and accept neutrality of Black Sea
Christians v. Muslims	Christians establish Latin Kingdom of Jerusalem
Christians v. Muslims	Muslims successfully resist Christian invasion
Christians v. Muslims	Christians capture Acre but fail to retake Jerusalem
Dutch v. Spanish	Dutch win independence from Spain
Royalists v. Parliamentarians	Parliament victory; eventual execution of Charles I and establishment of Protectorate

Name	Dates
Falklands War	1982
French Revolutionary Wars	1792–99
French Wars of Religion	1562–98
Gallic Wars	58–51 BC
Greek War of Independence	1821–28
Gulf War	1991
Hundred Years' War	1337–1453
Indian Mutiny	1857–59
Iran–Iraq War	1980–88
Iraq War	2003
Jacobite Rebellion	1745–46

Combatants	Outcome
Britain v. Argentina	Britain recaptures Falkland Islands from Argentinian invasion force
French v. neighbouring states	French repel invaders and invade neighbouring states
Catholics v. Huguenots	Catholicism firmly established
Romans (under Julius Caesar) v. Gauls	Caesar conquers Transalpine Gaul
Greeks, with aid of Britain, Russia and France v. Ottoman Empire	Greece wins independence
Iraq v. US-led UN forces	Iraqi invaders expelled from Kuwait
English v. French	English expelled from French possessions except Calais and Channel Islands
Indian rebels v. British	British rule re-established, with administration transferred from the East India Company to the British Crown
Iran v. Iraq	Inconclusive; Iraq eventually conceded disputed territory
Iraq v. US/British-led coalition forces	Saddam Hussein overthrown; Iraq occupied; new Iraqi government elected 2005
Jacobites v. Hanoverians	Jacobite cause suffers final military defeat

Name	Dates
Korean War	1950–53
Maori Wars	1845–48; 1860–72
Napoleonic Wars	1799–1815
Opium Wars access to China	1839–42; 1856–60
Peloponnesian War	431–404 BC
Peninsular War	1808–14
Persian Wars	490–479 BC
Pontiac's War	1763–66
Punic War (1st)	264–41 BC
Punic War (2nd)	218–01 BC
Punic War (3rd)	149–46 BC
Queen Anne's War	1702–13

Combatants	Outcome
North Korea (aided by China) v. South Korea (aided by UN forces)	North Korean invaders repelled
Maoris v. British settlers in New Zealand	Maoris lost territory but won ban against enforced sale of Maori land
France v. Britain, Prussia, Russia and Austria	Napoleon finally defeated at Waterloo
Britain v. China	British won increased trading
Sparta v. Athens	Sparta dominates Greece
British, Portuguese and Spanish v. French	French expelled from Spain
Persians v. Greek city-states	Greeks defeat Persian attempts to invade
Native American peoples v. British	Rebellion crushed by British
Rome v. Carthage	Rome conquers Carthaginian island of Sicily
Rome v. Carthage	Hannibal invades Italy but is ultimately expelled
Rome v. Carthage	Romans finally conquer and destroy Carthage
British v. French	British take control of Newfoundland, Acadia and Hudson's Bay

Name	Dates
Seven Years' War	1756–63
Six Day War	1967
Spanish Civil War	1936–39
Thirty Years' War	1618–48
Vietnam War	1964–75
War of 1812	1812–14
War of Jenkins' Ear	1739
War of the Pacific	1879–84
War of the Spanish Succession	1702–13

Combatants	Outcome
Britain, Prussia, Portugal v. France, Austria, Russia, Sweden, Saxony	Britain and Prussia dominant in Europe
Israel v. Egypt, Jordan and Syria	Israel defeats enemies in six days and occupies much territory
Spanish Republican government v. Nationalist rebels	Nationalists gain control
Initially European Protestants v. Catholics, eventually the German emperor v. vassal states	France ascendant in Europe; German states achieve sovereignty and religious toleration
North Vietnam v. South Vietnam (aided by USA and Australia)	North Vietnamese conquer South Vietnam
USA v. Britain	US attacks on Canada repulsed; US independence firmly established
Britain v. Spain	Subsumed into War of the Austrian Succession, 1740–48
Chile v. Peru and Bolivia	Chile gains territory
England, Holy Roman Empire and United Provinces (Netherlands) v. France and Spain	Bourbon succession in Spain confirmed

Name	Dates
Wars of the Roses	1455–85
World War I	1914–18
World War II	1939–45
Zulu War	1879

Combatants	Outcome
House of York v. House of Lancaster	Lancastrian king Henry VII united the warring houses by marrying a daughter of the Yorkist Edward IV
Allies (chiefly Britain, France, Russia, Italy, USA) v. Central Powers (chiefly Germany, Austria-Hungary and Turkey)	Germans lose territory in Europe and overseas colonies
Allies (chiefly Britain, USA and Russia) v. Axis Powers (chiefly Germany, Italy and Japan)	Germans and Japanese defeated
Zulus v. British	Military power of Zulus crushed

Geography

BEAUFORT SCALE

Scale No.	Description	Speed mph (kph)	Characteristics on land
0	Calm	Less than 1 (1)	Smoke goes straight up
1	Light air	1–3 (1–5)	Smoke blows in wind
2	Light breeze	4–7 (6–12)	Wind felt on face; leaves rustle
3	Gentle breeze	8–12 (13–20)	Light flag flutters; leaves in constant motion
4	Moderate breeze	13–18 (21–29)	Dust and loose paper blown. Small branches move
5	Fresh breeze	19–24 (30–39)	Small trees sway
6	Strong breeze	25–31 (40–50)	Hard to use umbrellas. Whistling heard in telegraph wires
7	Moderate gale	32–38 (51–61)	Hard to walk into. Whole trees in motion
8	Fresh gale	39–46 (62–74)	Twigs break off trees
9	Strong gale	47–54 (75–87)	Chimney pots and slates lost
10	Whole gale	55–63 (88–102)	Trees uprooted. Considerable structural damage
11	Storm	64–75 (103–120)	Widespread damage
12–17	Hurricane	over 75 (120)	Violent, massive damage

The measurement of wind speed.

Characteristics at sea
Sea like a mirror
Ripples formed, but without foam crests
Small wavelets. Crests glassy but do not break
Large wavelets. Crests begin to break. Foam glassy, scattered white horses
Small waves. Fairly frequent white horses
Moderate waves. Many white horses. Chance of spray
Large waves, extensive white foam crests. Probably spray
Sea leaps up. White foam from breaking waves begins to be blown in streaks along wind direction
Moderately high waves. Edges of crests begin to break into the spindrift. Foam blown in well-marked streaks along wind direction
High waves. Dense streaks of foam along wind direction. Crests topple, tumble and roll over. Spray may affect visibility
Very high waves with long overhanging crests. Foam is blown in great patches along wind direction. Surface takes on a general white appearance. Visibility affected
Exceptionally high waves. Sea completely covered with long white patches of foam lying along wind direction. Visibility affected
Air is filled with foam and spray. Sea completely white with driving spray. Visibility seriously affected

RICHTER AND MERCALLI SCALES

The magnitude of earthquakes is measured in units on the Richter Scale and their intensity on the Mercalli Scale.

Mercalli	Richter	Characteristics
1	less than 3.5	Only detected by seismograph
2	3.5	Only noticed by people at rest
3	4.2	Similar to vibrations from HGV
4	4.5	Felt indoors; rocks parked cars
5	4.8	Generally felt; awakens sleepers
6	5.4	Trees sway; causes some damage
7	6.1	Causes general alarm; building walls crack
8	6.5	Walls collapse
9	6.9	Some houses collapse; cracks appear in ground
10	7.3	Buildings destroyed; rails buckle
11	8.1	Most buildings destroyed; landslides
12	greater than 8.1	Total destruction of area

SHIPPING AREAS

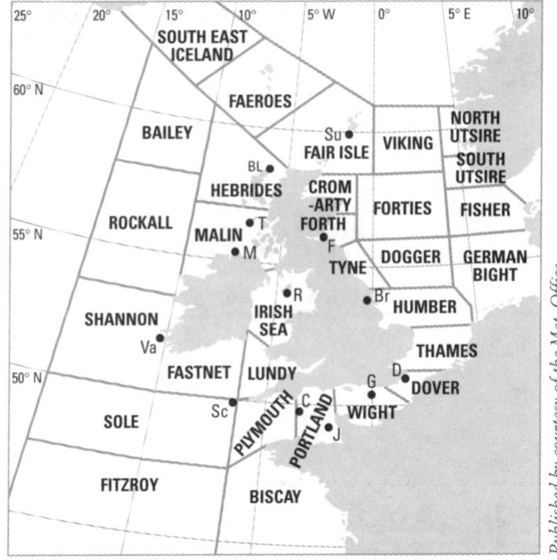

Published by courtesy of the Met. Office.

T	Tiree	**G**	Greenwich light vessel automatic ('Greenwich LV auto')
BL	Butt of Lewis	**C**	Channel
Su	Sumburgh	**Sc**	Scilly auto
F	Fifeness	**Va**	Valentia
Br	Bridlington	**R**	Ronaldsway
D	Dover	**M**	Malin Head
J	Jersey		

CONTINENTS OF THE WORLD

Name	Area (sq km)
Asia	45,036,492
America	42,495,751
Africa	30,343,578
Antarctica	12,093,000
Europe	9,908,599
Oceania	8,844,516

** Usually divided politically into North/Central and South America; North/Central America is 24,680,331 sq km*
*** Including European Russia*
**** Australia, New Zealand and non-Asian Pacific islands*

LARGEST ISLANDS

Name	Ocean	Area (sq km)
Greenland	Arctic	2,175,600
New Guinea	Pacific	808,510
Borneo	Pacific	745,561
Madagascar	Indian	587,040
Baffin	Arctic	507,451

LARGEST OCEANS

Name	Area (sq km)	Greatest depth (m)
Pacific	166,241,000	10,920
Atlantic	86,557,000	8,605
Indian	73,437,000	7,125
Arctic	9,485,000	5,400

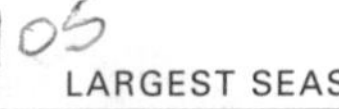

LARGEST SEAS

Name	Area (sq km)	Greatest depth (m)
South China	2,974,600	7,260
Caribbean	2,753,000	8,600
Mediterranean	2,503,000	5,100
Bering	2,226,100	3,930
Gulf of Mexico	1,542,985	3,505

LARGEST DESERTS

Name	Continent	Area (sq km)
Sahara	Africa	8,400,000
Australian	Australia	1,550,000
Arabian	Asia	1,300,000
Gobi	Asia	1,040,000
Kalahari	Africa	520,000

HIGHEST MOUNTAINS

Name (all in Himalayas)	Height (m)
Everest	8,848
K2	8,611
Kangchenjunga	8,586
Lhotse	8,516
Makalu	8,463

HIGHEST VOLCANOES (ACTIVE)

Name	Country	Height (m)
Gullatiri	Chile	6,060
Cotopaxi	Ecuador	5,897
Tupungatito	Chile	5,640
Lascar	Chile	5,590
Nevado del Ruiz	Colombia	5,400

HIGHEST WATERFALLS

Name	Country	Height (m)
Angel	Venezuela	979
Tugela	South Africa	850
Utigord	Norway	800
Monge	Norway	774
Mutarazi	Zimbabwe	762

LONGEST RIVERS

Name	Continent	Length (km)
Nile	Africa	6,695
Amazon	S America	6,516
Yangtze	Asia	6,380
Mississippi-Missouri	N America	5,969
Ob'-Irtysh	Asia	5,568

LARGEST LAKES

Name	Continent	Area (sq km)
Caspian Sea	Asia	371,000
Superior	N America	82,100
Victoria	Africa	68,800
Huron	N America	59,600
Michigan	N America	57,800

DEEPEST CAVES

Name	Country	Depth (m)
Reseau Jean Bernard	France	1,602
Shakta Pantjukhina	Georgia	1,508
Sistema del Trave	Spain	1,441
Aminakoateak	Spain	1,408
Snezhnaya	Georgia	1,370

LARGEST COUNTRIES (AREA)

Name	Area (sq km)
Russian Federation	17,075,400
Canada	9,984,670
USA	9,826,635
China	9,584,492
Brazil	8,514,879

LARGEST COUNTRIES (POPULATION)

Name	Population (2003 est)
China	1,289,161,000
India	1,065,462,000
USA	294,043,000
Indonesia	219,883,000
Brazil	178,470,000

SMALLEST COUNTRIES (AREA)

Name	Area (sq km)
Vatican City	0.5
Monaco	2.0
Nauru	21.0
Tuvalu	25.0
San Marino	61.0

SMALLEST COUNTRIES (POPULATION)

Name	Population (2003 est)
Vatican City	472
Tuvalu	11,000
Nauru	13,000
San Marino	28,000
Liechtenstein and Monaco (each)	34,000

MOST DENSELY POPULATED COUNTRIES WITH POPULATIONS OVER 10 MILLION

Name	People per sq km (2003)
Bangladesh	1,019
Taiwan	623
South Korea	480
Netherlands	389
India	348

Greenland is the least densely populated country with one person per 38.1 sq km; the UK has 241 people per sq km. Estimates put the world population at 6 billion, rising to 8.9 billion by 2050.

LARGEST CITIES

Name	Country	Population (2005)
Tokyo	Japan	35,327,000
Mexico City	Mexico	19,013,000
New York	USA	18,498,000
Mumbai	India	18,336,000
São Paulo	Brazil	18,333,000

LONGEST ROAD TUNNELS

Name	Country	Length (km)
Laerdal	Norway	24.51
St Gotthard	Switzerland	16.91
Arlberg	Austria	13.98
Hsuehshan	Taiwan	12.90
Fréjus	France/Italy	12.89

LONGEST RAIL TUNNELS

Name	Country	Length (km)
Seikan	Japan	53.90
Channel Tunnel	France/England	49.94
Moscow Metro, Belyaevo–Medvekov	Russia	30.60
London Underground, East Finchley–Morden	England	27.84
Oshimizu	Japan	22.17

LONGEST BRIDGES (MAIN SPAN)

Name	Country	Length (m)
Akashi Kaikyo	Japan	1990
Izmit Bay	Turkey	1668
Store Baelt	Denmark	1624
Humber	UK	1410
Jiangyin	China	1385

HIGHEST DAMS

Name	Country	Height (m)
Rogun	Tajikistan	335
Nurek	Tajikistan	300
Grande Dixence	Switzerland	285
Inguri	Georgia	272
Vaiont	Italy	262

BUSIEST PORTS

By volume	By number of containers
Singapore	Hong Kong
Rotterdam	Singapore
South Louisiana	Pusan, South Korea
Shanghai	Kaohsiung, Taiwan
Hong Kong	Rotterdam

BUSIEST INTERNATIONAL AIRPORTS

City	Name	Country	Passengers (millions per year)
Atlanta	Hartsfield	USA	75.9
Chicago	O'Hare	USA	66.5
London	Heathrow	UK	63.3
Tokyo	Haneda	Japan	61.1
Los Angeles	Los Angeles	USA	56.2

MAJOR CITIES AND THEIR RIVERS

City	River
Baghdad, Iraq	Tigris
Bangkok, Thailand	Chao Phrya
Bonn, Germany	Rhine
Bordeaux, France	Garonne
Bristol, UK	Avon
Budapest, Hungary	Danube
Cairo, Egypt	Nile
Christchurch, New Zealand	Avon
Cincinnatti, USA	Ohio
Dublin, Ireland	Liffey
Florence, Italy	Arno
Frankfurt, Germany	Main
Glasgow, UK	Clyde
Kiev, Ukraine	Dnieper
Leeds, UK	Aire
Limerick, Ireland	Shannon
Lisbon, Portugal	Tagus
London, UK	Thames
Memphis, USA	Mississippi
Moscow, Russia	Moskva

City	River
Newcastle, UK	Tyne
New York, USA	Hudson
Paris, France	Seine
Perth, Australia	Swan
Prague, Czech Republic	Vltava
Quebec, Canada	St Lawrence
Rome, Italy	Tiber
St Petersburg, Russia	Neva
Turin, Italy	Po
Vienna, Austria	Danube
Warsaw, Poland	Vistula
Washington DC, USA	Potomac

Religion

THE TEN COMMANDMENTS

Exodus 20: 1–17 (from the *Good News Bible*)

God spoke, and these were his words: 2 'I am the Lord your God
who brought you out of Egypt, where you were slaves.

3 'Worship no god but me.

4 'Do not make for yourselves images of anything in heaven or on earth or in the water under the earth.

5 Do not bow down to any idol or worship it, because I am the Lord your God and I tolerate no rivals. I bring punishment on those who hate me and on their descendants down to the third and fourth generation.

6 But I show my love to thousands of generations of those who love me and obey my laws.

7 'Do not use my name for evil purposes, for I, the Lord your God, will punish anyone who misuses my name.

8 'Observe the Sabbath and keep it holy.

9 You have six days in which to do your work,

10 But the seventh day is a day of rest dedicated to me. On that day no one is to work – neither you, your children, your slaves, your animals, nor the foreigners who live in your country.

11 In six days I, the Lord, made the earth, the sky, the sea, and everything in them, but on the seventh day I rested. That is why I, the Lord, blessed the Sabbath and made it holy.

Exodus 20: 1–17 *cont.*

12 'Respect your father and your mother, so that you may live a long time in the land that I am giving you.

13 'Do not commit murder.

14 'Do not commit adultery.

15 'Do not steal.

16 'Do not accuse anyone falsely.

17 'Do not desire another man's house; do not desire his wife, his slaves, his cattle, his donkeys, or anything else that he owns.'

THE BEATITUDES

Matthew 5:3–12 (from the *Good News Bible*)

3 'Happy are those who know they are spiritually poor; the Kingdom of heaven belongs to them!

4 Happy are those who mourn; God will comfort them!

5 Happy are those who are humble; they will receive what God has promised!

6 Happy are those whose greatest desire is to do what God requires; God will satisfy them fully!

7 Happy are those who are merciful to others; God will be merciful to them!

8 Happy are the pure in heart; they will see God!

9 Happy are those who work for peace; God will call them his children!

Matthew 5:3–12 *cont.*

10 Happy are those who are persecuted because they do what God requires; the Kingdom of heaven belongs to them!

11 Happy are you when people insult you and persecute you and tell all kinds of evil lies against you because you are my followers.

12 Be happy and glad, for a great reward is kept for you in heaven. This is how the prophets who lived before you were persecuted.

THE STATIONS OF THE CROSS

A devotional aid to meditation on the Passion of Christ.

1. Jesus is condemned to death.
2. Jesus bears his cross.
3. Jesus falls the first time.
4. Jesus meets his mother.
5. Jesus is helped by Simon.
6. Veronica wipes the face of Jesus.
7. Jesus falls a second time.
8. Jesus consoles the women of Jerusalem.
9. Jesus falls a third time.
10. Jesus is stripped of his garments.
11. Jesus is nailed to the cross.
12. Jesus dies on the cross.
13. Jesus is taken down from the cross.
14. Jesus is laid in the tomb.

THE TWELVE APOSTLES

Andrew	Peter (Simon)
James	John
Philip	Nathanael (Bartholomew)
Matthew (Levi)	Thomas
James (son of Alphaeus)	Judas (brother of James)
Judas Iscariot	Simon the Zealot

After the death of Judas Iscariot, the number was maintained at twelve by the election of Matthias.

THE FOUR LAST THINGS

Death	Judgment	Heaven	Hell

THE SEVEN SACRAMENTS

Baptism	Penance	Ordination
Confirmation	Anointing of the Sick	Matrimony
Eucharist		

THE SEVEN CHAMPIONS OF CHRISTENDOM

Name	Emblem
St George of England	Red cross on white ground
St Andrew of Scotland	Cross saltire gold on blue ground
St David of Wales	Dove
St Patrick of Ireland	Shamrock and snakes
St Denis of France	Carrying his severed head, witness to martyrdom
St James of Spain	Scallop shell
St Antony of Padua (Italy)	Lily, flowered cross and book

THE SEVEN FATHERS OF THE CHURCH

Early bishops and writers on doctrine.

- St Athanasius
- St Gregory of Nazianzus
- St John Chrysostom
- St John of Damascus
- St Basil of Caesarea
- St Gregory of Nyssa
- St Cyril of Alexandria

THE TEN PLAGUES OF EGYPT

1 Water turns to blood
2 Frogs
3 Lice, sand flies or fleas
4 Swarms of flies
5 Cattle die from disease
6 Boils and sores
7 Hail
8 Locusts
9 Darkness
10 Death of first-born

THE FOUR HORSEMEN OF THE APOCALYPSE

Revelation 6

Four riders whose arrival symbolizes the end of the world and the devastation and terror accompanying this event.

The rider of the White Horse carries a bow and wears a crown; he represents the Power of God triumphing over evil.

The rider of the fiery Red Horse carries a large sword and represents Bloodshed and War.

The rider of the Black Horse carries a pair of scales and represents Famine.

The rider of the Pale Horse is called Death and is closely followed by Hades; he represents Disease and Death.

THE TWELVE TRIBES OF ISRAEL

Genesis 29–30, 35

The twelve tribes, by tradition, take their roots from the twelve sons of Jacob.

Reuben	Asher
Judah	Joseph
Gad	Levi
Zebulun	Naphtali
Simeon	Issachar
Dan	Benjamin

THE SEVEN LAST PLAGUES

Revelation 16

1 Sores
2 Sea turns to blood
3 Rivers turn to blood
4 People scorched by intense heat of sun
5 Darkness
6 River Euphrates dries up
7 Earthquake

THE SEVEN CORPORAL WORKS OF MERCY

Food to the Hungry
Drink to the Thirsty
Clothing to the Naked
Harbouring the Stranger
Visiting the Sick
Ministering to Prisoners
Burying the Dead

SAINTS AND SAINTS' DAYS

The list on pages 120–25 shows a wide cross-section from the many hundreds of saints who are, or were, venerated on the days shown. It is not intended to represent the calendar of any particular denomination.

January

1 Abbot Clarus
2 Basil, Gregory
3 Geneviève
4 Roger of Ellant
5 Simeon Stylites
6 Melanius
7 Raymond of Peñafort
8 Lucian, Nathalan
9 Adrian of Canterbury
10 Peter Orseolo
11 Alexander
12 Benedict Biscop
13 Bishop Hilary
14 Felix of Nola
15 Ita
16 Bernard and his Companions
17 Antony the Abbot
18 Prisca
19 Canute IV, King of Denmark
20 Sebastian, Fabian
21 Agnes
22 Vincent of Saragossa
23 Emerentiana
24 Francis de Sales
25 Dwyn
26 Paula
27 John Chrysostom
28 Thomas Aquinas
29 Gildas
30 Aidan
31 John Bosco

February

1 Brigid of Ireland
2 Joan de Lestonnac
3 Blaise
4 John de Britto, Gilbert of Sempringham
5 Agatha
6 Amand
7 Apollonia
8 Jerome Emiliani
9 Teilo
10 Scholastica
11 Finnian
12 Julian the Hospitaller, Seven Servite Founders
13 Huna
14 Valentine
15 Sigfrid
16 Juliana
17 Finan
18 Colman of Lindisfarne
19 Mesrop
20 Ulric of Haselbury
21 Peter Damian
22 Margaret of Cortona
23 Polycarp
24 Montanus and Lucius
25 Walburga
26 Porphyry of Gaza
27 Gabriel Possenti
28 Oswald

March

1 David
2 Chad
3 Cunegund
4 Adrian of Nicomedia
5 Bishop Ciaran
6 Baldred
7 Perpetua and Felicity
8 John of God
9 Dominic Savio, Frances of Rome
10 John Ogilvie
11 Eulogius of Cordoba
12 Pope Gregory the Great
13 Gerald of Mayo
14 Matilda
15 Louise de Marillac
16 Boniface of Ross
17 Joseph of Arimathea, Patrick
18 Fra Angelico, Cyril of Jerusalem
19 Joseph
20 Cuthbert
21 Abbot Benedict
22 Zachary
23 Turibius
24 Catherine of Sweden
25 Dismas
26 Ludger
27 Rupert of Salzburg
28 Guntramnus
29 Gwladys
30 John Climacus
31 Benjamin

April

1 Hugh of Grenoble
2 Francis of Paola
3 Richard of Chichester
4 Benedict the Black
5 Vincent Ferrer
6 William of Eskill
7 John Baptist de la Salle
8 Walter of Pontoise
9 Waudru
10 Michael de Sanctis
11 Stanislaus
12 Pope Martin I
13 Guinoch
14 Tiburtius and Valerian
15 Ruadhan
16 Bernadette of Lourdes, Magnus of Orkney
17 Donnan
18 Apollonius the Apologist
19 Expeditus
20 Caedwalla, King of Wessex
21 Anselm
22 Theodore of Sykean
23 George
24 Ivo
25 Mark
26 Cletus
27 Zita
28 Peter Mary Chanel
29 Catherine of Siena
30 Adjutor

May

1 Peregrine Laziosi
2 Athanasius
3 Alexander and Eventius
4 Florian
5 Asaph
6 Adbert
7 John of Beverley
8 Victor Maurus
9 Pachomius
10 Cathal
11 Gengulf
12 Pancras
13 Andrew Fournet, Caradoc
14 Apostle Matthias
15 Dympna, Isidore the Farmer
16 Honoratus, John Nepomucen, Ubald
17 Paschal Baylon
18 Venantius, John I
19 Ivo of Kermartin, Pope Celestine V
20 Bernardino of Siena
21 Godric
22 Rita of Cascia
23 William of Rochester
24 David of Scotland
25 Venerable Bede, Gregory VII
26 Philip Neri
27 Augustine of Canterbury
28 Bernard of Montjoux
29 Bona
30 Ferdinand III of Castile
31 Petronilla

June

1 Nicomede
2 Erasmus (Elmo)
3 Charles Lwanga
4 Petroc, Joan of Arc
5 Boniface
6 Norbert
7 Colman of Dromore
8 William of York
9 Columba of Iona
10 Landerious of Paris
11 Barnabas
12 Ternan
13 Antony of Padua
14 Basil the Great
15 Vitus
16 John Francis Regis
17 Alban
18 Mark and Marcellian
19 Romuald
20 Adalbert of Magdeburg, Mary, Our Lady of Consolation
21 Aloysius
22 John Fisher, Thomas More
23 Agrippina
24 John the Baptist
25 Febronia
26 Anthelm
27 Cyril of Alexandria, Kyned
28 Austell
29 Paul, Peter
30 Erentrude

July

1 Oliver Plunkett, Serf
2 Otto
3 Thomas the Apostle
4 Elizabeth of Portugal
5 Modwenna
6 Maria Goretti
7 Hedda of Winchester
8 Bishop Killian
9 Everildis, Virgin Mary, Queen of Peace
10 The Seven Brothers
11 Drostan
12 John Gualbert
13 Henry II
14 Camillus de Lellis
15 Swithin
16 Helier
17 Kenelm
18 Edburga of Winchester
19 Gervase, Protase
20 Margaret (Marina)
21 Laurence of Brindisi
22 Mary Magdalene
23 Apollinaris
24 Gleb, Christina
25 James the Great, Christopher, Margaret
26 Anne
27 The Seven Sleepers of Ephesus
28 Samson
29 Martha
30 Abdon, Sennen
31 Ignatius of Loyola

August

1 Alphonsus Liguori
2 Theodota of Nicaea
3 Germanus of Auxerre
4 John Mary Vianney
5 Afra
6 Justua, Pastor
7 Pope Sixtus II
8 Cyriacus, Dominic
9 Emygdius
10 Lawrence
11 Clare
12 Attracta
13 Hippolytus, Cassian of Imola
14 Athanasia of Aegina
15 Mary the Virgin
16 Roch, Stephen of Hungary
17 Hyacinth
18 Helen
19 John Eudes
20 Bernard of Clairvaux
21 Pope Pius X
22 Symphorian
23 Rose of Lima
24 Bartholomew
25 Louis of France, Genesius the Comedian
26 Ninian
27 Monica
28 Augustine of Hippo
29 Sebbi
30 Felix, Adauctus
31 Raymond Nonnatus, Aidan of Lindisfarne

September

1 Fiacre, Giles
2 Brocard
3 Basilissa
4 Macnissi
5 Lawrence Giustiniani
6 Magnus of Fussen
7 Evurtius
8 Adrian, Natalia
9 Ciaran of Clonmacnoise
10 Nicholas of Tolentino
11 Deiniol
12 Guy of Anderlecht
13 Venerius
14 Notburga
15 Nicomedes
16 Cornelius, Ninian
17 Lambert
18 Joseph of Cupertino
19 Januarius
20 Eustace
21 Matthew
22 Maurice
23 Eunan, Adamnan
24 Gerard of Csanad
25 Finbarr
26 Cosmas and Damian, Cyprian
27 Vincent de Paul
28 Bernard of Feltre
29 Gabriel the Archangel, Michael the Archangel, Raphael the Archangel, Wenceslas
30 Jerome

October

1 Remigius
2 Leger
3 Hewald the Dark and Hewald the Fair
4 Francis of Assisi
5 Maurus, Placid
6 Faith (Foi), Bruno
7 Osith
8 Pelagia the Penitent
9 Denis, Bishop of Paris, John Leonardi
10 Paulinus of York
11 Canice (Kenneth)
12 Ethelburga of Barking
13 Edward the Confessor
14 Callistus I
15 Teresa of Avila
16 Gall, Margaret Mary
17 Ignatius of Antioch, Etheldreda (Audrey)
18 Luke
19 Paul of the Cross
20 Andrew of Crete
21 Fintan Munnu
22 Donatus of Fiesole
23 John Capistrano
24 Antony Claret
25 Crispin and Crispinian, Marnock, Margaret Clitherow
26 Eata
27 Frumentius
28 Simon, Jude
29 Colman of Kilmacduagh
30 Marcellus the Centurion
31 Bega (Bee)

November

1 All Saints' Day
2 Marcian (Cyrrhus)
3 Pirminus, Martin de Porres, Hubert
4 Charles Borromeo
5 Zachary, Elizabeth
6 Leonard of Noblac, Winnoc
7 Willibrord
8 Four Crowned Martyrs
9 Benignus (Benen)
10 Leo the Great, Andrew Avellino
11 Martin of Tours
12 Josaphat
13 Britius, Homobonus, Francis Xavier Cabrini
14 Lawrence O'Toole
15 Albert the Great, Fintan of Rheinau
16 Margaret of Scotland
17 Hugh of Lincoln, Gregory the Wonderworker
18 Mawes
19 Nerses I
20 Edmund
21 Albert of Louvain
22 Cecilia
23 Clement I, Columban
24 Chrysogonus
25 Catherine of Alexandria
26 John Berchmans
27 Maximus, Catherine Laboure
28 James of the March
29 Saturninus
30 Andrew

December

1 Eligius (Eloi)
2 Chromatius
3 Francis Xavier
4 Barbara, John Damascene
5 Birinus, Crispina
6 Nicholas of Bari
7 Ambrose
8 Budoc
9 Peter Fourier
10 Eulalia
11 Damasus, Corentin, Gentian
12 Jane Frances de Chantal
13 Lucy
14 John of the Cross
15 Mary di Rosa
16 Adelaide
17 Begga
18 Flannan
19 Anastasius I
20 Dominic of Silos
21 Peter Canisius
22 Chaeremon
23 John of Kanty, Thorlac
24 Delphinus
25 Anastasia, Eugenia
26 Stephen
27 John the Divine
28 The Holy Innocents
29 Thomas à Becket
30 Egwin
31 Sylvester

PATRON SAINTS OF THE BRITISH ISLES

1 March	David of Wales
17 March	Patrick of Ireland
23 April	George of England
30 November	Andrew of Scotland

PATRON SAINTS AND INTERCESSORS

Profession, condition, etc.	Saint	Date
Accountants	Matthew	21 September
Actors	Genesius the Comedian	25 August
Advertisers, advertising	Bernardino of Siena	20 May
Air stewards	Bona	29 May
Animals, sick	Nicholas of Tolentino	10 September
Animals, domestic	Antony the Abbot	17 January
Animals, danger from	Vitus	15 June
Apprentices	John Bosco	31 January
Archaeologists	Damasus	11 December
Archers	Sebastian	30 January
Architects	Thomas the Apostle	3 July
Armies, soldiers	Maurice	22 September
Artists	Luke	18 October
Astronauts	Joseph of Cupertino	18 September
Astronomers	Dominic	8 August
Asylums, mental	Dympna	15 May
Babies	Maximus	27 November
Bakers	Honoratus	16 May
Bankers	Matthew	21 September

Profession, condition, etc.	Saint	Date
Barbers	Cosmas and Damian	26 September
Bee-keepers	Bernard of Clairvaux	20 August
Birds	Gall	16 October
Blacksmiths	Eligius (Eloi)	1 December
Blind people	Thomas the Apostle	3 July
Book-keepers	Matthew	21 September
Booksellers, book trade	John of God	8 March
Boys, young	Dominic Savio	9 March
Breast-feeding	Basilissa	3 September
Brewers	Amand	6 February
Bricklayers	Stephen	26 December
Brides	Nicholas of Bari	6 December
Bridges	John Nepomucen	16 May
Broadcasters	Gabriel the Archangel	29 September
Builders	Thomas the Apostle	3 July
Business people	Homobonus	13 November
Butchers	Luke	18 October
Cabinet makers	Joseph	19 March
Cake makers	Honoratus	16 May
Cancer sufferers	Peregrine Laziosi	1 May
Cemetery caretakers	Joseph of Arimathea	17 March
Charitable societies	Vincent de Paul	27 September
Chemists (pharmacists)	Cosmas and Damian	26 September
Childbirth	Raymond Nonnatus	31 August
Childless women	Anne	26 July
Children	Nicholas of Bari	6 December
Children, desire for	Rita of Cascia	22 May
Children, illegitimate	John Francis Regis	16 June
Christian people, young	Aloysius	21 June
Clergy	Gabriel Possenti	27 February

Profession, condition, etc.	Saint	Date
Clothworkers	Homobonus	13 November
Coffin-bearers	Joseph of Arimathea	17 March
Colic	Erasmus (Elmo)	2 June
Colleges	Thomas Aquinas	28 January
Comedians	Vitus	15 June
Construction workers	Thomas the Apostle	3 July
Contagious diseases	Roch	16 August
Cooks	Lawrence	10 August
Craftsmen and -women	Eligius (Eloi)	1 December
Criminals, condemned	Dismas	25 March
Crops, protection of	Magnus of Fussen	6 September
Customs officers	Matthew	21 September
Dancers	Vitus	15 June
Deaf people	Francis de Sales	24 January
Death	Michael the Archangel	29 September
Death, happy	Joseph	19 March
Death, sudden	Andrew Avellino	10 November
Degree candidates	Joseph of Cupertino	18 September
Dentists	Apollonia	7 February
Devils, possession by	Cyriacus	8 August
Difficult situations	Eustace	20 September
Diplomatic services	Gabriel the Archangel	29 September
Disabled, physically	Giles	1 September
Disasters	Geneviève	3 January
Diseases, eye	Raphael the Archangel	29 September
Diseases, nervous	Dympna	15 May
Doctors	Luke	18 October
Dog bites	Ubald	16 May
Doubters	Joseph	19 March
Drought	Geneviève	3 January

Profession, condition, etc.	Saint	Date
Drowning, death by or danger from	Adjutor	30 April
Dying, the	Benedict	21 March
Earthquakes	Emygdius	9 August
Ecologists, ecology	Francis of Assisi	4 October
Eczema	Antony the Abbot	17 January
Editors	John Bosco	31 January
Education	Martin de Porres	3 November
Embroiderers	Clare	11 August
Emigrants	Francis Xavier Cabrini	13 November
Engineers	Ferdinand III of Castile	30 May
Epilepsy	Dympna	15 May
Examination candidates	Joseph of Cupertino	18 September
Falsely accused people	Raymond Nonnatus	31 August
Farmers	Isidore the Farmer	15 May
Farm workers	Benedict	21 March
Fathers	Joseph	19 March
Fever	Geneviève	3 January
Fire, danger from	Agatha	5 February
Fishermen	Peter	29 June
Flood	Gregory the Wonderworker	17 November
Florists and flower growers	Rose of Lima	23 August
Flying	Joseph of Cupertino	18 September
Foresters	John Gualbert	12 July
Garage workers	Eligius (Eloi)	1 December
Gardeners	Fiacre	1 September
Girls, teenage	Maria Goretti	6 July
Glaziers	Lucy	13 December
Goldsmiths	Eligius (Eloi)	1 December
Grave-diggers	Joseph of Arimathea	17 March

Profession, condition, etc.	Saint	Date
Grocers	Michael the Archangel	29 September
Haemorrhage	Lucy	13 December
Hairdressers	Cosmas and Damian	26 September
Harvests	Antony of Padua	13 June
Headaches	Denis, Bishop of Paris	9 October
Health inspectors	Raphael the Archangel	29 September
Hernia sufferers	Cathal	10 May
Hoarseness	Bernardino of Siena	20 May
Hopeless cases	Jude	28 October
Horses	Eligius (Eloi)	1 December
Horse-riders	Martin of Tours	11 November
Horticulturalists	Fiacre	1 September
Hospitals	John of God	8 March
Housewives	Martha	29 July
Infertility	Rita of Cascia	22 May
Innkeepers	Gentian	11 December
Insanity	Dympna	15 May
Invalids	Roch	16 August
Jewellers	Eligius (Eloi)	1 December
Joiners	Joseph	19 March
Journalists	Francis de Sales	24 January
Journeys, safe	Christopher	25 July
Judges	Ivo of Kermartin	16 May
Justice, social	Martin de Porres	3 November
Juvenile offenders	Dominic Savio	9 March
Lame people	Giles	1 September
Lawyers	Raymond of Peñafort	7 January
Learning	Catherine of Alexandria	25 November
Librarians, libraries	Jerome	30 September
Lighthouse keepers	Venerius	13 September

Profession, condition, etc.	Saint	Date
Lightning, protection against	Magnus of Fussen	6 September
Lost articles	Antony of Padua	13 June
Lovers	Valentine	14 February
Magistrates	Ferdinand III of Castile	30 May
Mariners	Francis of Paola	2 April
Maritime pilots	Nicholas of Bari	6 December
Marriages, unhappy	Gengulf	11 May
Married women	Monica	27 August
Medical profession	Cosmas and Damian	26 September
Merchants	Homobonus	13 November
Metalworkers	Eligius (Eloi)	1 December
Midwives	Raymond Nonnatus	31 August
Migrants	Francis Xavier Cabrini	31 November
Miners	Barbara	4 December
Missions	Francis Xavier	3 December
Mothers	Monica	27 August
Motorcyclists	Mary, Our Lady of Castellazzo	Unfixed
Motorists	Frances of Rome	9 March
Mountaineers	Bernard of Montjoux	28 May
Music	Cecilia	22 November
Naval officers	Francis of Paola	2 April
Navigators	Francis of Paola	2 April
Neighbourhood watch schemes	Sebastian	20 January
Nervous diseases	Vitus	15 June
Notaries	Luke	18 October
Nurses	Camillus de Lellis	14 July
Old people	Mary, Our Lady of Consolation	20 June
Painters (artists)	Fra Angelico	18 March
Paratroopers	Michael the Archangel	29 September

Profession, condition, etc.	Saint	Date
Parenthood	Rita of Cascia	22 May
Park keepers	John Gualbert	12 July
Pawnbrokers	Bernard of Feltre	28 September
People in authority	Ferdinand III of Castile	30 May
Pets	Antony the Abbot	17 January
Philatelists	Gabriel the Archangel	29 September
Philosophers, philosophy	Catherine of Alexandria	25 November
Pilgrims	Nicholas of Bari	6 December
Poets	Columba of Iona	9 June
Policemen and -women	Michael the Archangel	29 September
Poor people	Antony of Padua	13 June
Possession by devils	Cyriacus	8 August
Postal workers	Gabriel the Archangel	29 September
Preachers	John Chrysostom	27 January
Pregnant women	Margaret (Marina)	20 July
Priests	John Mary Vianney	4 August
Printers	John of God	8 March
Prison officers	Hippolytus	13 August
Prisoners	Leonard of Noblac	6 November
Procrastination (against)	Expeditus	19 April
Publishers	John the Divine	27 December
Quantity surveyors	Thomas the Apostle	3 July
Radio	Gabriel the Archangel	29 September
Radiologists, radiotherapists	Michael the Archangel	29 September
Rain, excessive	Geneviève	3 January
Rheumatism sufferers	James the Great	25 July
Sailors	Erasmus (Elmo)	2 June
Scholars	Thomas Aquinas	28 January
Scientists	Albert the Great	15 November
Sculptors	Luke	18 October

Profession, condition, etc.	Saint	Date
Secretaries	Genesius the Comedian	25 August
Security forces	Michael the Archangel	29 September
Security guards	Matthew	21 September
Short-sightedness	Clarus	1 January
Shorthand writers, stenographers	Cassian of Imola	13 August
Sick people	John of God	8 March
Signals, military	Gabriel the Archangel	29 September
Silversmiths	Eligius (Eloi)	1 December
Singers	Cecilia	22 November
Skiers	Bernard of Montjoux	28 May
Skin diseases	Antony the Abbot	17 January
Slander	John Nepomucen	16 May
Sleepwalkers	Dympna	15 May
Snakebites	Pirminus	3 November
Social justice	Martin de Porres	3 November
Social workers	John Francis Regis	16 June
Soldiers	Martin of Tours	11 November
Souls in purgatory	Nicholas of Tolentino	10 September
Stomach pains	Erasmus (Elmo)	2 June
Stonemasons	Four Crowned Martyrs	8 November
Storms, protection against	Vitus	15 June
Students	Thomas Aquinas	28 January
Students, female	Catherine of Alexandria	25 November
Students, young	John Berchmans	26 November
Swimmers	Adjutor	30 April
Tailors, dressmakers	Homobonus	13 November
Tax officials	Matthew	21 September
Taxi drivers	Fiacre	1 September
Teachers	John Baptist de la Salle	7 April

Profession, condition, etc.	Saint	Date
Telecommunications	Gabriel the Archangel	29 September
Television	Clare	11 August
Theatre	Genesius the Comedian	25 August
Theft, protection against	Dismas	25 March
Thieves, danger from	Leonard of Noblac	6 November
Throat infections	Blaise	3 February
Toothache	Apollonia	7 February
Tradesmen and -women	Homobonus	13 November
Travellers	Christopher	25 July
Undertakers	Dismas	25 March
Unmarried women	Nicholas of Bari	6 December
Urgent situations	Expeditus	19 April
Vermin, protection against	Magnus of Fussen	6 September
Veterinary surgeons	Eligius (Eloi)	1 December
Waiters, waitresses	Martha	29 July
War victims (non-combatants)	Mary, Queen of Peace	9 July
Water, danger from	Florian	4 May
Widows	Paula	26 January
Wine merchants, wine trade	Amand	6 February
Workers	Joseph	19 March
Writers	Francis de Sales	24 January
Young people	Raphael the Archangel	29 September

LARGEST RELIGIONS*

Religion	Worshippers (millions)
Christianity	1,955.2 (981 Roman Catholic, 404 Protestant, 218 Orthodox, 69 Anglican, 282 other)
Islam	1,126.3 (83% Sunnites, 16% Shi'ites, 1% other)
Hinduism	793.1 (70% Vaishnavites, 25% Shaivites)
Buddhism	325.3 (56% Mahayana, 38% Theravada, 6% Tantrayana)
Sikhism	19.5
Judaism	13.9
Confucianism	6.2
Baha'ism	5.8
Jainism	4.9
Shintoism	2.9

* *Excludes tribal/folk religions and shamanism*

TYPES OF CROSS

ankh

avellane

Calvary

Celtic

cross clechée

Ansated

cross crosslet

cross fitchée

cross fleury

cross formée

cross fourchée

cross gringolée

cross moline

cross pommée

Greek

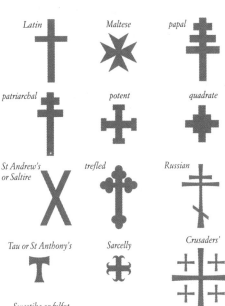

Latin

Maltese

papal

patriarchal

potent

quadrate

St Andrew's or Saltire

trefled

Russian

Tau or St Anthony's

Sarcelly

Crusaders'

Swastika or fylfot (derived from the pagan sunwheel)

Cross of Lorraine

POPES OF THE ROMAN CATHOLIC CHURCH

Note: This list does not include anti-popes.

c.42 Peter
c.67 Linus
c.76 Anacletus
c.88 Clement I
c.99 Evaristus
c.107 Alexander I
c.115 Sixtus I
c.125 Telephorus
c.136 Hyginus
c.140 Pius I
c.155 Anicetus
c.166 Soterus
175 Eleutherius
189 Victor I
199 Zephyrinus
217 Calistus I
222 Urban I
230 Pontian
235 Anterus
236 Fabian
251 Cornelius
253 Lucius I
254 Stephen I
257 Sixtus II
259 Dionysius
269 Felix I
275 Eutychian
283 Caius
296 Marcellinus
308 Marcellus I
310 Eusebius
311 Melchiades
314 Sylvester I
336 Mark
337 Julius I
352 Liberius
366 Damasus I
384 Siricius
399 Anastasius I
401 Innocent I
417 Zosimus
418 Boniface I
422 Celestine I
432 Sixtus III
440 Leo I (the Great)
461 Hilarius
468 Simplicius
483 Felix III (or II)
492 Gelasius I
496 Anastasius II
498 Symmachus
514 Hormisdas
523 John I
526 Felix IV
530 Boniface II
533 John II
535 Agapitus I
536 Silverius
537 Vigilius
556 Pelagius II
561 John III
574 Benedict I
578 Pelagius II
590 Gregory I (the Great)

604 Sabinian
607 Boniface III
608 Boniface IV
615 Deusdedit (Adeodatus I)
619 Boniface V
625 Honorius I
640 Severinus
640 John IV
642 Theodore I
649 Martin I
654 Eugenius I
657 Vitalian
672 Adeodatus II
676 Donus
678 Agatho
682 Leo II
684 Benedict II
685 John V
686 Conon
687 Sergius I
701 John VI
705 John VII
708 Sisinnius
708 Constantine
715 Gregory II
731 Gregory III
741 Zachary
752 Stephen II
752 Stephen III
757 Paul I
768 Stephen IV
772 Adrian I
795 Leo III
816 Stephen V
817 Paschal I
824 Eugenius II
827 Valentine
827 Gregory IV
844 Sergius II
847 Leo IV
855 Benedict III
858 Nicholas I
867 Adrian II
872 John VIII
882 Marinus I
884 Adrian III
885 Stephen VI
891 Formosus
896 Boniface VI
896 Stephen VII
897 Romanus
897 Theodore II
898 John IX
900 Benedict IV
903 Leo V
904 Sergius III
911 Anastasius III
913 Lando
914 John X
928 Leo VI
928 Stephen VIII
931 John XI
936 Leo VII
939 Stephen IX
942 Marinus II
946 Agapitus II
955 John XII
963 Leo VIII
964 Benedict V
965 John XIII

973 Benedict VI
974 Benedict VII
983 John XIV
985 John XV
996 Gregory V
999 Sylvester II
1003 John XVII*
1004 John XVIII
1009 Sergius IV
1012 Benedict VIII
1024 John XIX
1032 Benedict IX
1045 Gregory VI
1046 Clement II
1047 Benedict IX
1048 Damasus II
1049 Leo IX
1055 Victor II
1057 Stephen X
1059 Nicholas II
1061 Alexander II
1073 Gregory VII
1086 Victor III
1088 Urban II
1099 Paschal II
1118 Gelasius II
1119 Callistus II
1124 Honorius II
1130 Innocent II
1143 Celestine II
1144 Lucius II
1145 Eugenius III
1153 Anastasius IV
1154 Adrian IV
1159 Alexander III
1181 Lucius III
1185 Urban III
1187 Gregory VIII
1187 Clement III
1191 Celestine III
1198 Innocent III
1216 Honorius III
1227 Gregory IX
1241 Celestine IV
1243 Innocent IV
1254 Alexander IV
1261 Urban IV
1265 Clement IV
1271 Gregory X
1276 Innocent V
1276 Adrian V
1276 John XXI†
1277 Nicholas III
1281 Martin IV
1285 Honorius IV
1288 Nicholas IV
1294 Celestine V
1294 Boniface VIII
1303 Benedict XI
1305 Clement V
1316 John XXII
1334 Benedict XII
1342 Clement VI
1352 Innocent VI
1362 Urban V
1370 Gregory XI
1378 Urban VI
1389 Boniface IX
1404 Innocent VII
1406 Gregory XII

1417	Martin V	1644	Innocent X
1431	Eugenius IV	1655	Alexander VII
1447	Nicholas V	1667	Clement IX
1455	Callistus III	1670	Clement X
1458	Pius II	1676	Innocent XI
1464	Paul II	1689	Alexander VIII
1471	Sixtus IV	1691	Innocent XII
1484	Innocent VIII	1700	Clement XI
1492	Alexander VI	1721	Innocent XIII
1503	Pius III	1724	Benedict XIII
1503	Julius II	1730	Clement XII
1513	Leo X	1740	Benedict XIV
1522	Adrian VI	1758	Clement XIII
1523	Clement VII	1769	Clement XIV
1534	Paul III	1775	Pius VI
1550	Julius III	1800	Pius VII
1555	Marcellus II	1823	Leo XII
1555	Paul IV	1829	Pius VIII
1559	Pius IV	1831	Gregory XVI
1566	Pius V	1846	Pius IX
1572	Gregory XIII	1878	Leo XIII
1585	Sixtus V	1903	Pius X
1590	Urban VII	1914	Benedict XV
1590	Gregory XIV	1922	Pius XI
1591	Innocent IX	1939	Pius XII
1592	Clement VIII	1958	John XXIII
1605	Leo XI	1963	Paul VI
1605	Paul V	1978	John Paul I
1621	Gregory XV	1978	John Paul II
1623	Urban VIII	2005	Benedict XVI

**John XVI was an 'anti–pope' (997–8) during the reign of Gregory V.*
† In fact only the twentieth John but crowned John XXI because a fifteenth John was once thought to have existed before the real John XV.

ARCHBISHOPS OF CANTERBURY

597	Augustine	1052	Stigand
604	Laurentius	1070	Lanfranc
619	Mellitus	1093	Anselm
624	Justus	1114	Ralph d'Escures
627	Honorius	1123	William de Corbeil
655	Deusdedit	1139	Theobald
668	Theodore	1162	Thomas à Becket
692	Boerhtweald	1174	Richard (of Dover)
731	Tatwine	1185	Baldwin
735	Nothelm	1193	Hubert Walter
740	Cuthbeorht	1207	Stephen Langton
761	Breguwine	1229	Richard le Grant
765	Jaenbeorht	1234	Edmund Rich
793	Aethelheard	1245	Boniface of Savoy
805	Wulfred	1273	Robert Kilwardby
832	Feologild	1279	John Pecham
833	Ceolnoth	1294	Robert Winchelsey
870	Aethelred	1313	Walter Reynolds
890	Plegmund	1328	Simon Mepeham
914	Aethelhelm	1333	John Stratford
923	Wulfhelm	1349	Thomas Bradwardine
942	Oda	1349	Simon Islip
959	Aefsige	1366	Simon Langham
959	Beorhthelm	1368	William Whittlesey
960	Dunstan	1375	Simon Sudbury
c.988	Athelgar	1381	William Courtenay
990	Siggeric Serio	1396	Thomas Arundel
995	Aelfric	1398	Roger Walden
1005	Aelfheah	1414	Henry Chichele
1013	Lyfing	1443	John Strafford
1020	Aethelnoth	1452	John Kemp
1038	Eadsige	1454	Thomas Bourchier
1051	Robert of Jumièges	1486	John Morton

1501 Henry Dean
1503 William Warham
1533 Thomas Cranmer*
1556 Reginald Pole
1559 Matthew Parker
1576 Edmund Grindal
1583 John Whitgift
1604 Richard Bancroft
1611 George Abbot
1633 William Laud
1660 William Juxon
1663 Gilbert Sheldon
1678 William Sancroft
1691 John Tillotson
1695 Thomas Tenison
1716 William Wake
1737 John Potter
1747 Thomas Herring
1757 Matthew Hutton
1758 Thomas Secker
1768 Frederick Cornwallis
1783 John Moore
1805 Charles Sutton
1828 William Howley
1848 John Sumner
1862 Charles Longley
1868 Archibald Tait
1883 Edward Benson
1896 Frederick Temple
1903 Randall Davidson
1928 Cosmo Lang
1942 William Temple
1945 Geoffrey Fisher
1961 Arthur Ramsey
1974 Donald Coggan
1980 Robert Runcie
1991 George Carey
2002 Rowan Williams

**Supported Henry VIII in his claims to be supreme head of the Church of England, thus severing links with Rome. Condemned for heresy in Queen Mary's reign and burned at the stake in Oxford in 1556.*

BOOKS OF THE BIBLE

Protestant Canon
Old Testament
Genesis
Exodus
Leviticus
Numbers
Deuteronomy
Joshua
Judges
Ruth
1 Samuel
2 Samuel
1 Kings
2 Kings
1 Chronicles
2 Chronicles
Ezra
Nehemiah
Esther
Job
Psalms
Ecclesiastes
Song of Solomon

Roman Catholic Canon
Old Testament
Genesis
Exodus
Leviticus
Numbers
Deuteronomy
Joshua (Josue)
Judges
Ruth
1 Samuel (1 Kings)
2 Samuel (2 Kings)
1 Kings (3 Kings)
2 Kings (4 Kings)
1 Chronicles (1 Paralipomenon)
2 Chronicles (2 Paralipomenon)
Ezra (1 Esdras)
Nehemiah (2 Esdras)
Tobit (Tobias)
Judith
Esther
Job
Psalms
Proverbs
Ecclesiastes
Song of Solomon (Canticle of Canticles)
The Wisdom of Solomon (Wisdom)

Protestant Canon
Old Testament *cont.*

Isaiah
Jeremiah
Lamentations
Ezekiel
Daniel
Hosea
Joel
Amos
Obadiah
Jonah
Micah
Nahum
Habakkuk
Zephaniah
Haggai
Zechariah
Malachi

Roman Catholic Canon
Old Testament *cont.*

Sirach (Ecclesiasticus)
Isaiah
Jeremiah
Lamentations
Baruch
Ezekiel (Ezechiel)
Daniel
Hosea (Osee)
Joel
Amos
Obadiah (Abdias)
Jonah (Jonas)
Micah (Micheas)
Nahum
Habakkuk (Habacuc)
Zephaniah (Sophonias)
Haggai (Aggeus)
Zechariah (Zacharias)
Malachi (Malachias)
1 Maccabees
(1 Machabees)
2 Maccabees
(2 Machabees)

Protestant Canon
New Testament

Matthew
Mark
Luke
John

Roman Catholic Canon
New Testament

Matthew
Mark
Luke
John

Protestant Canon
New Testament *cont.*
The Acts of the Apostles
Romans
1 Corinthians
2 Corinthians
Galatians
Ephesians
Philippians
Colossians
1 Thessalonians
2 Thessalonians
1 Timothy
2 Timothy
Titus
Philemon
Hebrews
James
1 Peter
2 Peter
1 John
2 John
3 John
Jude
Revelation

Roman Catholic Canon
New Testament *cont.*
The Acts of the Apostles
Romans
1 Corinthians
2 Corinthians
Galatians
Ephesians
Philippians
Colossians
1 Thessalonians
2 Thessalonians
1 Timothy
2 Timothy
Titus
Philemon
Hebrews
James
1 Peter
2 Peter
1 John
2 John
3 John
Jude
Revelation (Apocalypse)

Protestant Canon
Apocrypha
The First Book of Esdras
The Second Book of Esdras
Tobit

Roman Catholic Canon
Apocrypha
1 (3) Esdras
2 (4) Esdras
Tobit

Protestant Canon Apocrypha *cont.*	**Roman Catholic Canon Apocrypha** *cont.*
Judith	Judith
The Rest of the Chapters of the Book of Esther	Additions to Esther
The Wisdom of Solomon	The Wisdom of Solomon
Ecclesiasticus or the Wisdom of Jesus, Son of Sirach	Sirach
Baruch	Baruch
A Letter of Jeremiah	The Letter of Jeremiah
The Song of the Three Holy Children	The Prayer of Azariah and the Song of the Three Young Men
Daniel and Susanna	Susanna
Daniel, Bel and the Snake	Bel and the Dragon
The Prayer of Manasseh	The Prayer of Manasseh
The First Book of the Maccabees	1 Maccabees
The Second Book of the Maccabees	2 Maccabees

JEWISH TEXTS

The Law (Pentateuch)	The Prophets	The Writings
Genesis	Joshua	Psalms
Exodus	Judges	Proverbs
Leviticus	Samuel	Job
Numbers	Kings	Song of Solomon

The Law (Pentateuch)	The Prophets	The Writings
Deuteronomy	Isaiah	Ruth
	Jeremiah	Lamentations
	Ezekiel	Malachi
	Hosea	Ecclesiastes
	Joel	Esther
	Amos	Daniel
	Obadiah	Ezra
	Jonah	Nehemiah
	Micah	Chronicles
	Nahum	
	Habakkuk	
	Zephaniah	
	Haggai	
	Zechariah	

THE KORAN

Chapters of the Koran.

1 Entitled, The Preface or Introduction
2 Entitled, The Cow
3 Entitled, The Family of Imran
4 Entitled, Women
5 Entitled, The Table
6 Entitled, Cattle
7 Entitled, Al Araf
8 Entitled, The Spoils
9 Entitled, The Declaration of Immunity
10 Entitled, Jonas
11 Entitled, Hud
12 Entitled, Joseph
13 Entitled, Thunder
14 Entitled, Abraham
15 Entitled, Al Hejr
16 Entitled, The Bee
17 Entitled, The Night Journey

18 Entitled, The Cave
19 Entitled, Mary
20 Entitled, T.H.
21 Entitled, The Prophets
22 Entitled, The Pilgrimage
23 Entitled, The True Believers
24 Entitled, Light
25 Entitled, Al Forkan
26 Entitled, The Poets
27 Entitled, The Ant
28 Entitled, The Story
29 Entitled, The Spider
30 Entitled, The Greeks
31 Entitled, Lokman
32 Entitled, Adoration
33 Entitled, The Confederates
34 Entitled, Saba
35 Entitled, The Creator
36 Entitled, Y.S.
37 Entitled, Those who Rank themselves in Order
38 Entitled, S.
39 Entitled, The Troops
40 Entitled, The True Believer
41 Entitled, Are Distinctly Explained
42 Entitled, Consultation
43 Entitled, The Ornaments of Gold
44 Entitled, Smoke
45 Entitled, The Kneeling
46 Entitled, Al Ahkaf
47 Entitled, Mohammed
48 Entitled, The Victory
49 Entitled, The Inner Apartments
50 Entitled, K.
51 Entitled, The Dispersing
52 Entitled, The Mountain
53 Entitled, The Star
54 Entitled, The Moon
55 Entitled, The Merciful
56 Entitled, The Inevitable
57 Entitled, Iron
58 Entitled, She who Disputed
59 Entitled, The Emigration
60 Entitled, She who is Tied
61 Entitled, Battle Array
62 Entitled, The Assembly
63 Entitled, The Hypocrites
64 Entitled, Mutual Deceit
65 Entitled, Divorce
66 Entitled, Prohibition
67 Entitled, The Kingdom
68 Entitled, The Pen
69 Entitled, The Infallible
70 Entitled, The Steps
71 Entitled, Noah

72 Entitled, The Genii
73 Entitled, The Wrapped Up
74 Entitled, The Covered
75 Entitled, The Resurrection
76 Entitled, Man
77 Entitled, Those which are Sent
78 Entitled, The News
79 Entitled, Those who Tear Forth
80 Entitled, He Frowned
81 Entitled, The Folding Up
82 Entitled, The Cleaving in Sunder
83 Entitled, Those who Give Short Measure of Weight
84 Entitled, The Rending in Sunder
85 Entitled, The Celestial Signs
86 Entitled, The Star which Appeareth by Night
87 Entitled, The Most High
88 Entitled, The Overwhelming
89 Entitled, The Daybreak
90 Entitled, The Territory
91 Entitled, The Sun
92 Entitled, The Night
93 Entitled, The Brightness
94 Entitled, Have We not Opened
95 Entitled, The Fig
96 Entitled, Congealed Blood
97 Entitled, Al Kadr
98 Entitled, The Evidence
99 Entitled, The Earthquake
100 Entitled, The War-Horses which Run Swiftly
101 Entitled, The Striking
102 Entitled, The Emulous Desire of Multiplying
103 Entitled, The Afternoon
104 Entitled, The Slanderer
105 Entitled, The Elephant
106 Entitled, Koreish
107 Entitled, Necessaries
108 Entitled, Al Cawthar
109 Entitled, The Unbelievers
110 Entitled, Assistance
111 Entitled, Abu Laheb
112 Entitled, The Declaration of God's Unity
113 Entitled, The Daybreak
114 Entitled, Men

THE FIVE PILLARS OF ISLAM

These are the five duties that every Muslim is expected to carry out.

- Profession of the faith
- Formal prayer
- Fasting during the month of Ramadan
- The giving of alms to the poor
- Pilgrimage to Mecca

SIKHISM

Sikhism is a monotheistic religion that was founded in India by Guru Nanak (1469–1539). The sacred text is called the Adi Granth, and initiated Sikhs are known collectively as the Khalsa. Sikhs identify themselves by the Five Ks.

Kachera	Traditional short trousers
Kangha	A comb
Kara	A steel bangle
Kesh	Uncut hair and beard
Kirpan	Short sword

HINDU TEXTS

Hinduism has no single volume representing its doctrines. Of the many sacred writings which go to make up its fundamental beliefs, the following are considered to be the most significant.

The Vedas

Rig-Veda	Yajur-Veda
Sama-Veda	Atharva-Veda

The Puranas

Ramayana

Mahabharata (including the Bhagavadgita)

The Manu Smriti (Code of Manu)

BUDDHIST (PALI) TEXTS

1 Canonical Literature

The Three Baskets of Tripitaka

Vinaya Pitaka – Basket of Discipline

Sutta Pitaka – Basket of Discourses

Abhidharma Pitaka – Basket of the Higher Dharma

Note: Additional scriptures have been added by the various Buddhist schools

2 Non-canonical Literature

a Chronicles

Dipavamsa – 'Island Chronicle'

Mahavamsa – 'Great Chronicle'

Culavamsa – 'Little Chronicle'

Mahabodhivamsa – 'Chronicle of the Bodhi-Tree'

Thupavamsa – 'Chronicle of the Stupa'
Daathavamsa – 'Chronicle of the Sacred Relic' (i.e. the Buddha's tooth)
Sasanavamsa – 'Chronicle of the Religion'

b Commentaries on Canonical Texts
These are too numerous to list, but among the most important are those composed by Buddhaghosa on the Vinaya Pitaka, the Digha Nikaya and on the first book of the Abhidharma Pitaka.

c Compendiums or manuals of Buddhist life and philosophy based on Canonical Texts
Again, too numerous to list but works such as the Visuddhimagga, the Malindapanha and the Abhidhammatthasangaha are the most important.

PRINCIPAL GODS

GREEK

Name of Deity	Representing/symbolizing
Zeus	God of gods
Poseidon	The sea; father of rivers and fountains
Hades	The underworld; death
Apollo	The sun
Hermes	Messenger and herald of the gods
Ares	War
Hephaestus	Fire
Dionysus	Wine
Uranus	Heaven
Hera	Goddess of the heavens; patroness and protector of marriage
Demeter	Abundance of corn and fruit; agriculture
Hestia	Hearth and home
Artemis	Moon, hunting, chastity
Athene	Wisdom

Greek *cont.*

Name of Deity	Representing/symbolizing
Aphrodite	Love and beauty
Hebe	Youth
Gaea	Earth

ROMAN

Name of Deity	Representing/symbolizing
Jupiter	God of gods
Neptune	The sea
Pluto	The underworld; death
Apollo	The sun
Mercury	Messenger of the gods
Mars	War
Vulcan	Fire
Bacchus	Wine
Coelus	Heaven
Saturn	Abundance
Juno	Queen of the heavens; guardian of women
Ceres	Agriculture
Vesta	Hearth and home
Diana	Hunting; chastity
Minerva	Wisdom
Venus	Love; beauty
Terra	Earth

Note: Saturn's day = Saturday

NORSE

Name of Deity	Representing/symbolizing
Odin	Chief god; war, wisdom, poetry, prophecy, magic
Thor	Thunder
Balder	Sun
Hermod	Messenger of the gods

Norse *cont.*

Name of Deity	**Representing/symbolizing**
Tyr	War; athletic activities. A hero, the killer of Game, the Hellhound
Forseti	Guardian of justice
Bragi	Poetry, wisdom and eloquence; welcomed dead warriors to the underworld
Heimdal	Light; guardian of the Bifrost, the rainbow bridge leading to Valhalla
Hodur	Blind son of Odin; god of night
Vidar	Forests; 'the silent god'
Uller	Hunting
Vali	Son of Odin
Thjazi	Winter
Holler	Death
Mimir	Custodian of the Fountain of Wisdom
Ymir	Frost giant
Kari	Son of Ymir; controls air, storms
Hler	Son of Ymir; controls the sea
Logi	Son of Ymir; controls fire
Aegir	Giant of the seashore
Frey	Fruitfulness; sender of sunshine and rain
Frigga	Earth, air, conjugal love
Fulla	Mother goddess
Sjofna	Love
Lofn	Reconciliation of separated lovers
Vara	Punishment of unfaithful lovers
Syn	One of Frigga's attendants
Gerda	The frozen earth
Freyja	Fertility, love
Jord	Earth
Saga	History
Iduna	Spring; guardian of the apples which rejuvenated the gods

Norse *cont.*

Name of Deity	Representing/symbolizing
Bil	Child-deity; associated with waning moon
Siguna	Truth
Nanna	Wife of Balder; possessor of magic ring
Gefjon	Protection of girls who died unmarried
Snotra	Wisdom
Gna	Messenger of the goddesses
Hel	The dead
Eir	Healing
Ran	Storms and the sea; drew the drowned under the waves in her net

Note: Odin's day (Anglo-Saxon 'Woden') = Wednesday; Thor's day = Thursday; Freyja's day = Friday

Other Figures

The three Norns represent Fate: Urda represents the past, Verdandi the present and Skuld the future. The thirteen Valkyries rode through the air and over the sea to select those who were to die in battle and whose souls were then transported to Valhalla where they enjoyed a perfect and everlasting existence, feasting and recounting their deeds of valour.

The elves were tiny creatures who plagued or helped mankind according to whim. The dwarfs lived in the heart of the hills and were metalworkers and jewellers. The giants stole summer and brought winter in its place. One of these was Hresvelgr who produced winds and storms by moving his wings.

EGYPTIAN

Name of Deity	Representing/symbolizing
Osiris	Earth, sky; principle of good
Set	Darkness; principle of evil
Ra	Sun
Shu	Dry atmospheres
Tefnut	Waters above the heavens
Name of Deity	Representing/symbolizing
Keb	Earth, vegetation
Pthah	Artisan of the world (made sun, moon, earth); holds world in his hands
Horus	Light
Anubis	The dead; art of embalming
Thoth	Art of letters; registrar and recorder of the underworld
Apis	Beast-god in form of a bull
Khem	Generation and production
Ranno	Gardens
Serapis	Healing
Isis	Earth, moon; has limitless powers
Maut	Mother of gods; mistress of sky
Athor	Sky, rising and setting sun; love and beauty
Maat	Truth; law and order
Mu	Light
Nephthys	The dead; personification of dusk
Neith	Upper heaven or ether
Anouke	War
Babastis	Gentle rays of the sun
Sekhet	Burning heat of the sun
Sphinx	Wisdom; earth's abundance
Anquet	Fertilizing waters of the Nile
Nut	Childbirth; nursing

Science

THE HUMAN SKELETON

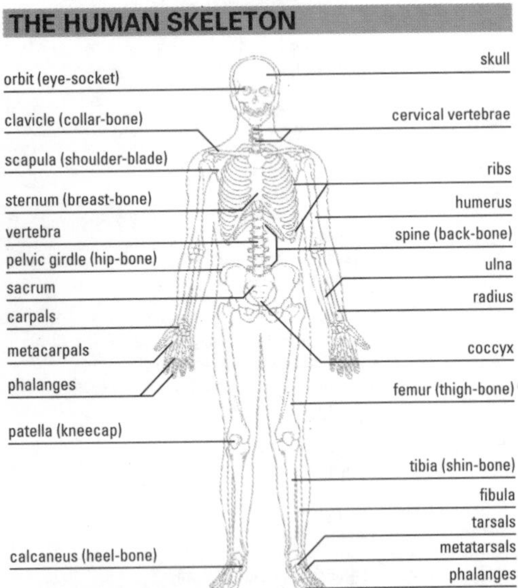

THE SEVEN LIFE PROCESSES

An organism is deemed to be living if it shows the following processes:

movement	respiration	sensitivity	growth
reproduction	excretion	nutrition	

TISSUE TYPES

The body is made up of cells, which form tissues. An organ can be defined as a structure that contains at least two different types of tissue functioning together for a certain purpose. Tissues are of four main types:

epithelial tissue
continuous sheets of cells that line organs, protecting them, holding them in place and keeping them separate; examples include the lining of the mouth and stomach, and the outer layer of the skin

connective tissue
adds support and structure; usually their strength comes from fibrous strands of the protein collagen; examples include tendons, ligaments, cartilage, bone and the inner layers of skin, while blood can also be considered a form of connective tissue

muscle tissue
a specialized tissue that can contract; contains the proteins actin and myosin that slide past one another and allow movement

nerve tissue
generates and conducts electrical signals transmitted from the brain down the spinal cord to the relevant part of the body

THE NINE ORGAN SYSTEMS

cardiovascular (circulatory) system
includes: heart, arteries, veins, capillaries, blood
purpose: transporting nutrients, hormones and wastes around the body
digestive system
includes: mouth, salivary glands, pharynx, oesophagus, stomach, small intestine, large intestine, anus, pancreas, liver, gall bladder
purpose: breaking down food into nutrients that can be absorbed into the blood
endocrine system
includes: thyroid, parathyroid, thymus, pituitary, pancreas, gonads (ovaries/testes)
purpose: sending chemical signals through the body using hormones to regulate processes such as nutrient absorption, growth and maturation
excretory system
includes: kidneys, urethra, bladder, lungs, liver, intestines, sweat glands
purpose: regulating the body's metabolic balance by filtering out wastes, toxins and excess water or nutrients
muscular system
includes: muscles, tendons, ligaments
purpose: providing movement and protection, and controlling the passage of materials through some organs
nervous system
includes: brain, spinal cord, nerves, eyes, ears, nose, tongue, skin

purpose: sending electrical signals through the body to control processes such as movement, digestion and circulation

reproductive system

includes: (females) ovary, uterus, vagina, mammary glands; (males) testes, prostate gland, penis

purpose: producing and transporting cells (sperm, ovaries) that allow the organism to reproduce

respiratory system

includes: lungs, trachea, bronchi (air passages), pharynx, larynx, nasal cavities

purpose: allowing gases to pass in and out of the blood, absorbing oxygen and expelling carbon dioxide

skeletal system

includes: bones, cartilage, marrow, tendons, ligaments

purpose: providing structure for the body and allowing it to move, protecting internal organs and providing attachment sites for them

To these the following are sometimes added:

integumentary system

includes: skin, hair, nails, sub-cutaneous tissue

purpose: various purposes, including protection, temperature regulation and sensory reception

lymphatic (immune) system:

includes: spleen, lymph nodes, thymus, lymphatic vessels, white blood cells, T- and B- cells

purpose: removing harmful microbes and viruses from the body, as well as fat and excess fluids

GEOLOGICAL TABLE

Ages in millions of years (estimated).

Era	Period	Epoch	Time
Cenozoic	Quaternary	Holocene (recent)	c.0.01
		Pleistocene	c.2
	Tertiary	Pliocene	c.5
		Miocene	25
		Oligocene	40
		Eocene	55
		Palaeocene	65
Mesozoic	Cretaceous		135
	Jurassic		200
	Triassic		250
Palaeozoic	Permean		290
	Carboniferous		350
	Devonian		400
	Silurian		440
	Ordovician		500
	Cambrian		600
Precambrian	Proterozoic		2500
	Archaeozoic		3000
	Azoic		4000
			4500

Major Events	Animal and Plant Life
Ice Ages affect N Hemisphere temperature; sea retreats	End of Ice Age, development of man; vegetation – Arctic forms to present size
Shallow seas in Europe	Mammals spread, early man
Thick unconsolidated clays	Whales and apes
Deposits on Great Plains	Modern mammals
Alpine-Himalayan mountain building	First horses, elephants
	Early mammals
Chalk deposited in deep seas over Europe and Asia; marginal seas in N America	End of dinosaurs, flowering plants spread
Deep sea in Europe, swamps in N America	Giant dinosaurs, first birds
W Europe – shallow sea, red sands in N America	Small dinosaurs, first mammals
Shallow seas, continental deposits, mountain building	
Shallow seas over continents, extensive mountain building, coal formation	Forests formed coal, first reptiles
Erosion, large shallow seas, sandstones, thick shales	First forests and land animals, amphibians
Erosion, low areas resubmerged, mountain building in N America, Europe and Siberia	First land plants
Europe and N America mainly submerged; continental uplift	First fishes
Europe mainly submerged; N America submerged with large shallow areas	
	Sea animals without backbones, seaweeds
	First primitive plants and animals
	Earliest known rocks
	Earth formed

CHEMICAL ELEMENTS

Name	Atomic Number	Symbol	Atomic Weight
Actinium	89	Ac	227.0278*
Aluminium	13	Al	26.98154
Americium	95	Am	243.0614*
Antimony	51	Sb	121.75
Argon	18	Ar	39.948
Arsenic	33	As	74.9216
Astatine	85	At	209.9870*
Barium	56	Ba	137.33
Berkelium	97	Bk	247.0703*
Beryllium	4	Be	9.01218
Bismuth	83	Bi	208.9804
Bohrium	107	Bh	262.1229*
Boron	5	B	10.81
Bromine	35	Br	79.904
Cadmium	48	Cd	112.41
Caesium	55	Cs	132.9054
Calcium	20	Ca	40.08
Californium	98	Cf	251.0796*
Carbon	6	C	12.011
Cerium	58	Ce	140.12
Chlorine	17	Cl	35.453
Chromium	24	Cr	51.996
Cobalt	27	Co	58.9332
Copper	29	Cu	63.546
Curium	96	Cm	247.703*
Dubnium	105	Db	261.1087*
Dysprosium	66	Dy	162.5
Einsteinium	99	Es	254.0880*

Name	Atomic Number	Symbol	Atomic Weight
Erbium	68	Er	167.26
Europium	63	Eu	151.96
Fermium	100	Fm	257.0951*
Fluorine	9	F	18.9984*
Francium	87	Fr	223.0197*
Gallium	31	Ga	69.72
Gadolinium	64	Gd	157.25
Germanium	32	Ge	72.59
Gold	79	Au	196.9665
Hafnium	72	Hf	178.49
Hassium†	108	Hs	265.1302
Helium	2	He	4.0026
Holmium	67	Ho	164.9304
Hydrogen	1	H	1.0079
Iodine	53	I	126.9045
Indium	49	In	114.82
Iridium	77	Ir	192.22
Iron	26	Fe	55.847
Krypton	36	Kr	83.8
Lanthanum	57	La	138.9055
Lawrencium	103	Lr	260.105*
Lead	82	Pb	207.19
Lithium	3	Li	6.941
Lutetium	71	Lu	174.97
Magnesium	12	Mg	24.305
Manganese	25	Mn	54.938
Meitnerium	109	Mt	266.1376*
Mendelevium	101	Md	258.099*
Mercury	80	Hg	200.59
Molybdenum	42	Mo	95.94

Name	Atomic Number	Symbol	Atomic Weight
Neodymium	60	Nd	144.24
Neon	10	Ne	20.179
Neptunium	93	Np	237.0482*
Nickel	28	Ni	58.71
Niobium	41	Nb	92.9064
Nitrogen	7	N	14.0067
Nobelium	102	No	259.101*
Oxygen	8	O	15.9994
Osmium	76	Os	190.2
Palladium	46	Pd	106.4
Phosphorus	15	P	30.97376
Platinum	78	Pt	195.09
Plutonium	94	Pu	244.0642*
Polonium	84	Po	208.9824*
Potassium	19	K	39.0983
Praseodymium	59	Pr	140.9077
Promethium	61	Pm	144.9128*
Protactinium	91	Pa	231.0359
Radium	88	Ra	226.0254*
Radon	86	Rn	222.0176*
Rhenium	75	Re	186.207
Rhodium	45	Rh	102.9055
Rubidium	37	Rb	85.4678
Ruthenium	44	Ru	101.07
Rutherfordium	104	Ru	261
Samarium	62	Sm	150.35
Scandium	21	Sc	44.9559
Seaborgium†	106	Sg	263.1182*
Selenium	34	Se	78.96
Sodium	11	Na	22.98977

Name	Atomic Number	Symbol	Atomic Weight
Silicon	14	Si	28.0855
Silver	47	Ag	107.868
Strontium	38	Sr	87.62
Sulphur	16	S	32.064
Tantalum	73	Ta	180.9479
Technetium	43	Tc	96.9064*
Tellurium	52	Te	127.6
Terbium	65	Tb	158.9254
Thallium	81	Tl	204.37
Thorium	90	Th	232.0381
Thulium	69	Tm	168.9342
Tin	50	Sn	118.69
Titanium	22	Ti	47.9
Tungsten	74	W	183.85
Ununbium†	112	Uub	277
Ununnilium†	110	Uun	269
Unununium†	111	Uuu	272
Uranium	92	U	238.029*
Vanadium	23	V	50.9414
Xenon	54	Xe	131.3
Ytterbium	70	Yb	173.04
Yttrium	39	Y	88.9059
Zinc	30	Zn	65.381
Zirconium	40	Zr	91.22

** The atomic weight of the isotope with the longest known half-life.*
† Names being reviewed by the International Union of Pure and Applied Chemistry (IUPAC).

PERIODIC TABLE

Calcium (C), gold (Au) and hydrogen (H) are chemical elements which are examples of basic chemical substances. They cannot be broken down into simpler forms. This gives each element distinctive properties. The periodic table gives information about all the 112 known elements. (Elements 104 to 112 have been produced artificially.)

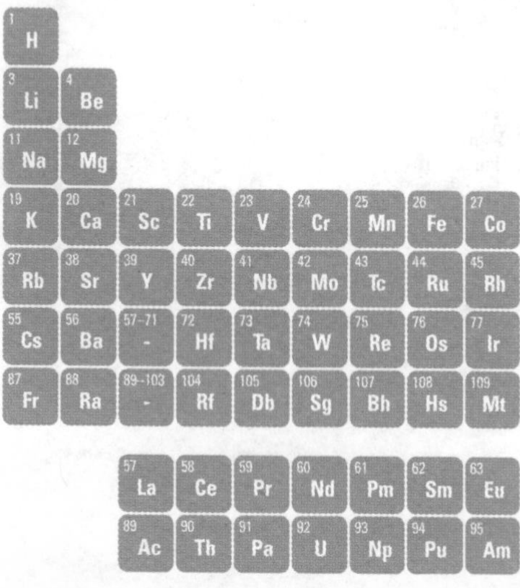

The periodic table was devised in 1869 by the Russian chemist Dmitri Mendeleyev. The table groups elements into seven lines or periods. As we read from left to right the elements become less metallic. The elements in each vertical group have similar chemical properties. Further information about the elements is given on pages 164–7.

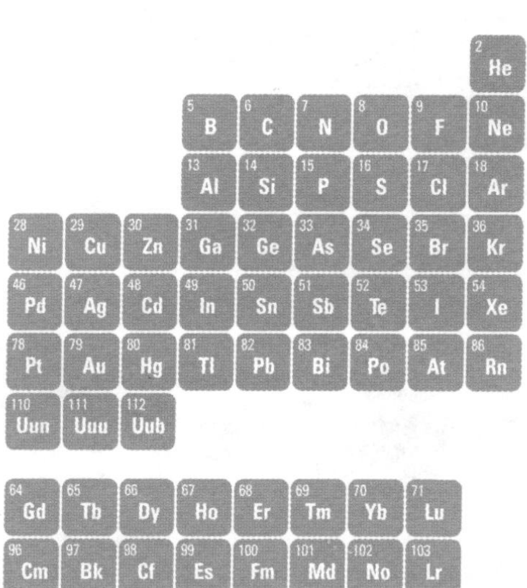

MOHS' HARDNESS SCALE

This scale was invented by Friedrich Mohs (1773–1839), a German mineralogist, and is used for testing the hardness of materials by comparing them with the ten standard minerals.

Mineral	Simple hardness test	Mohs' Hardness
Talc	Crushed by fingernail	1.0
Gypsum	Scratched by fingernail	2.0
Calcite	Scratched by copper coin	3.0
Fluorspar	Scratched by glass	4.0
Apatite	Scratched by a penknife	5.0
Feldspar	Scratched by quartz	6.0
Quartz	Scratched by a steel file	7.0
Topaz	Scratched by corundum	8.0
Corundum	Scratched by a diamond	9.0
Diamond		10.0

GEMSTONES

Mineral	Colour	Mohs' Hardness
Agate	Brown, red, blue, green, yellow	7.0
Alexandrite	Green	7.5
Amethyst	Violet	7.0
Aquamarine	Sky blue, greenish blue	7.5
Beryl	Green, blue, pink	7.5
Bloodstone	Green with red spots	7.0

Mineral	Colour	Mohs' Hardness
Carnelian	Red, reddish-yellow	7.0
Chalcedony	All colours	7.0
Chrysoprase	Apple green	7.0
Citrine	Yellow	7.0
Diamond	Colourless; tints of various colours	10.0
Emerald	Green	7.5
Garnet	Red and other colours	6.5-7.25
Jade	Green, whitish, mauve, brown	7.0
Lapis lazuli	Deep blue	5.5
Malachite	Dark green banded	3.5
Moonstone	Whitish with blue shimmer	6.0
Onyx	Various colours with straight coloured bands	7.0
Opal	Black, white, orange-red, rainbow	6.0
Pearl	Pale greyish-white, black	–
Peridot	Pale green	–
Ruby	Red	9.0
Sapphire	Blue and other colours	9.0
Sardonyx	Reddish brown, white bands	7.0
Serpentine	Red and green	3.0
Soapstone	White, possibly marked by impurities	2.0
Sunstone	Whitish-reddish-brown with golden particles	6.0
Topaz	Blue, green, pink, yellow, colourless	8.0
Tourmaline	Brown-black, blue, pink, red, violet-red, yellow, green	7.5
Turquoise	Greenish-grey, sky blue	6.0
Zircon	All colours	7.5

SCIENTIFIC LAWS

Physics – Gases

Scientist	Dates
Boyle, Robert	1627–91
Charles, Jacques	1746–1823
Dalton, John	1766–1844
Henry, William	1774–1836
Avogadro, Amedeo	1776–1856
Gay-Lussac, Joseph Louis	1778–1850
Graham, Thomas	1805–69

Physics – Fluids

Scientist	Dates
Archimedes	287–212 BC
Pascal, Blaise	1623–62

Description
The volume of a given mass of gas is inversely proportional to its pressure, temperature remaining constant.
The volume of a given mass of gas is directly proportional to its absolute temperature, pressure remaining constant.
Law of Partial Pressures. In a mixture of gases, the pressure of a component gas is the same as if it alone occupied the space. Atomic Theory. Elements are composed of atoms that can combine in definite proportions to form compounds.
The weight of gas dissolved by a liquid is proportional to the gas pressure.
Equal volumes of all gases at the same temperature contain the same quantity of molecules.
When gases react, they do so in volumes which bear a simple ratio to one another and to the volume of the product if it is a gas, temperature and pressure remaining constant.
The rates of diffusion of gases are inversely proportional to the square roots of their densities.

Description
Principle of Displacement. When a body is totally or partially immersed in a fluid it experiences an upthrust equal to the weight of the fluid displaced. Principle of Flotation. When a body floats it displaces a weight of fluid equal to its own weight.
In a fluid, pressure applied at any point is transmitted equally throughout it.

Bernoulli, Daniel	1700–82
Blagden, Charles	1748-1820

Physics – Energy

Scientist	Dates
Hooke, Robert	1635–1703
Ohm, Georg Simon	1787–1854
Faraday, Michael	1791–1867
Doppler, Christian	1803–53
Lenz, H F E	1804–65
Planck, Max	1858–1947

Physics – Relativity

Scientist	Dates
Einstein, Albert	1879–1955

When the speed of a fluid increases the pressure in the fluid decreases, and when speed decreases pressure increases.

At constant pressure and for dilute solutions, the elevation of boiling point or the depression of freezing point of the solvent is directly proportional to the concentration of a given solute.

Description

The extension produced in a spring is proportional to the applied force.

Voltage (V) in volts between ends of a conductor equals product of current (I) in amps flowing through it and its resistance (R): $V=IR$

1. The mass of a given element liberated during electrolysis is directly proportional to the magnitude of the steady current used to the time for which the current passes.
2. The masses of different elements liberated by the same quantity of electricity are directly proportional to their chemical equivalents.

The apparent change in frequency of sound or light caused by movement of a source with respect to the observer.

When a wire moves in a magnetic field, the electric current induced in the wire generates a magnetic field that tends to oppose the movement.

Quantum Theory. Light and other forms of energy are given off as separate packets (quanta) of energy.

Description

Theory of Relativity. Mass and energy are related by the equation $E=mc^2$, where E is the energy produced by a mass change m, and c is the speed of light.

Physics – Motion

Scientist	Dates
Newton, Sir Isaac	1642–1727

Chemistry

Scientist	Dates
Le Chatelier, H L	1850–1936

Mathematics

Scientist	Dates
Pythagoras	580–500 BC

Description

Laws of Motion:

1. A body will continue in its state of rest or uniform velocity unless acted on by an unbalanced force.
2. The rate of change of momentum of a body varies directly to the force causing the change and takes place in the same direction as the force.
3. If a body A exerts a force F on a body B then B exerts a force -F on A; that is, action and reaction are equal and opposite.
4. If no external force acts on a system in a particular direction then the total momentum of the system in that direction remains unchanged.

Law of Gravitation. The force of the attraction between two given particles is inversely proportional to the square of their distance apart.

Description

If a system in chemical equilibrium is subjected to a disturbance it tends to change in a way which opposes the disturbance.

Description

In a right-angled triangle, the square on the longest side (the hypotenuse) is equal to the sum of the squares on the other two sides.

INVENTIONS

Invention/Discovery	Year	Name and/or Country
Aeroplane	1903	Orville and Wilbur Wright
Aerosol can	1926	Erik Rotheim
Airship, rigid	1906	Ferdinand von Zeppelin
Anemometer	1644	Robert Hooke
Aspirin	1899	Felix Hoffmann
Atomic bomb	1945	Frisch, Bohr, Peierls
Bakelite	1907	Leo Baekeland
Balloon	1783	Joseph and Etienne Montgolfier
Barometer	1643	Evangelista Torricelli
Battery, electric	c.1799	Volta and Galvani
Bicycle	1839	Kirkpatrick Macmillan
Calculator, pocket	1971	Kilby, van Tassell, Merryman
Camera obscura	1560	Giovanni Battista della Porta
Canning, food	1810	Nicholas Appert
Canning, petfood	1865	James Spratt
Car, diesel	1895	Rudolf Diesel
Car, fuel-cell powered	1996	Daimler-Benz
Car, gas	1807	Isaac de Rivez
Car, internal combustion engine	1884	Gottlieb Daimler
Car, petrol engine	1886	Karl Benz
Cats' eyes	1934	Percy Shaw
Cellophane	1908	J E Brandenburger
Centigrade scale	c.1741	Anders Celsius
Chloroform	1847	James Young Simpson
Choc-ice	1922	C K Nelson
Christmas card	1843	John Calcott Horsley
Coca Cola	1886	John Pemberton
Cocoa powder	1828	Conraad Johannes van Houten
Coinage	650–600 BC	Asia Minor
Coffee, instant	1937	Nestlé
Compact disc	1979	Philips, Sony

Invention/Discovery	Year	Name and/or Country
Compact disc interactive player	1992	Philips
Compass	1269	Petrus Peregrinus de Maricourt (some authorities cite China c.1000/1100)
Computer, electronic	1948	Frederick Williams
Computer, personal	1981	IBM
Concorde supersonic aeroplane	1969	Britain/France
Concrete	133 BC	Romans
Contact lens	1887	Eugen A Frick
Contact lens (plastic corneal lens)	1956	Norman Bier
Contraceptive, oral	1956	Gregory Pincus (first large-scale experiments)
Cornflakes	1894	J & W Kellogg
Credit card	1950	Ralph Schneider
Crossbow	400 BC	China
Crossword puzzle	1913	Arthur Wynne
Dictionary	600 BC	Mesopotamia (written in Akkadian)
Digital camera	1994	Apple
Digital video (or versatile) disc (DVD) player	1996	Philips
Disc brake	1902	Frederick Lanchester
Doll, talking	1823	Johann Maelzel
Dye, hair	1909	Eugene Schueller
Dye, synthetic	1856	William H Perkin
Dynamite	1866	Alfred Nobel
Dynamo	1871	Zénobe Gramme
Elastoplast	1928	Smith & Nephew Ltd
Electrocardiograph	1903	Wilhelm Einthoven
Engine, jet	1937	Frank Whittle
Escalator	1892	Reno and Wheeler
Fan, rotary	180	China
Film, photographic	1888	George Eastman

Invention/Discovery	Year	Name and/or Country
Fire extinguisher	1762	Dr Godfrey (also attrib. to George Manby, 1816)
Geiger counter	1913	Rutherford and Geiger
Gimbals	180	China
Glassmaking	1500 BC	Mesopotamia
Gramophone record	1887	Emile Berliner
Gun, machine (flintlock)	1718	James Puckle
Gunpowder	221 BC	China
Hairdryer	1890	Alexandre Godefoy
Handkerchiefs, disposable	1924	Kimberley Clark Co
Helicopter	1907	Louis and Jacques Breguet
Hovercraft	1959	Christopher Cockerell
Inflatable swimming aid	880 BC	King Assur-Nasir Apli II of Assyria
Ink	2500 BC	China
Insulin	1921	Discovered by Paulesco
Iron, domestic steam	1938	Edmund Schreyer
Iron, electric	1882	Henry W Seeley
Kaleidoscope	1816	David Brewster
Kirby hairgrip	1893	Hindes
Kite	400 BC	China
Lamp, halogen	1980	Philips
Laser	1960	Charles Townes
Lawnmower	1831	Edward Budding , design; Ferrabee, manufacture
Lego	1955	Ole and Godtfried Kirk Christiansen
Lightbulb	1877	Edison and Swan
Lighthouse	285 BC	Pharos, near Alexandria
Lightning conductor	1752	Benjamin Franklin
Locomotive, diesel	1912	Sulzer Co
Locomotive, steam	1804	Richard Trevithick
Loudspeaker	1924	Rice-Kellogg
Magnifying glass	1250	Roger Bacon
Margarine	1869	Hippolyte Mège-Mouriés
Mars bar	1920	Frank Mars
Meccano	1900	Frank Hornby

Invention/Discovery	Year	Name and/or Country
Metal detector	1931	Gerhard Fisher
Meteorological map	1686	Edmund Halley
Microchip	1959	Kilby and Robert Noyce
Micrometer	1638	William Gascoigne
Microprocessor	1971	Intel Corporation
Microphone	1878	David Edward Hughes
Microscope, compound	1590	Hans and Zacharias Janssen
Milking machine	1862	L O Colvin
Mobile phone	1973	Martin Cooper, Motorola
Monopoly	1933	Charles Darrow
Motorcycle	1885	Gottlieb Daimler
Neon lighting	c.1910	Georges Claude
Nivea creme	1911	Paul Beiersdorf
Nylon	1937	Wallace Carruthers
Ovaltine	1904	George Wander
Oven, microwave	1945	Percy le Baron Spencer
Pacemaker, cardiac	1958	Ake Senning
Padlock	c.1380	Inventor unknown
Pan, non-stick	1954	Marc Gregoire
Paper, toilet	1857	Joseph Cayetty
Paper, writing	100	Cai Lun
Paperclip	1900	Johann Waaler
Parachute	1797	André Jacques Garnerin
Parking meter	1935	Carlton C Magee
Pen, ballpoint	1938	Laszlo and George Biro
Pen, fibre tip	1963	Pentel Co
Pen, fountain	1884	Lewis Edson Waterman
Penicillin	1928	Alexander Fleming
Pentium 64-bit processor	1993	Intel Co
Perspex	1934	Rowland Hill
Photography (metal)	1826	Joseph Niépce
Photography (paper)	1835	William Fox Talbot
Pistol	1540	Camillo Vettelli
Post-it notes	1981	Spencer Sylver
Pressure cooker	1680	Denis Papin

Invention/Discovery	Year	Name and/or Country
Printing (clay characters)	1041	Bi Shang
Printing (movable type)	1447	Johannes Gensfleisch zur Laden zum Gutenberg
Pump, steam	1698	Thomas Savery
Radar	1922	A Taylor and L Young
Radiator	1897	Wilhelm Maybach
Radio	1901	Guglielmo Marconi
Radio broadcast (public)	1906	Reginald Aubrey Fessenden
Recorder, video	1956	Ampex Corporation
Refrigerator	1862	James Harrison
Revolver	1835	Samuel Colt
Rifle barrel	1520	August Kotter
Saccharine	1879	Constantin Fahlberg
Safety lamp, miner's	1816	Humphry Davy
Safety pin	1849	Walter Hunt
Scotch tape	1925	Richard Drew, US; introduced to UK from France as Sellotape
Scrabble	1948	James Brunot
Seat belt, car	1903	Gustave Desiré Liebau
Secateurs	1815	Bertrand de Moleville
Sewer, city	600 BC	Cloaca Maxima, Rome
Sewing machine	1830	Barthélemy Thimonnier
Sextant	1757	John Campbell
Soda-water maker	1820	Charles Cameron
Spark plug	1885	Etienne Lenoir
Spectacles	1281	Salvino degli Armati and Alessandro della Spina
Spinning Jenny	1768	Thomas Higgs; perfected by James Hargreaves
Spirit level	1662	Jean de Melchisedech Thevenot
Stainless steel	1913	Harry Brearley
Stapler	1868	Charles Henry Gould
Submarine	1776	David Bushnell
Tape recorder	1935	AEG GmbH
Tea bags	1919	Joseph Krieger

Invention/Discovery	Year	Name and/or Country
Teddy bear	1902	Morris Mitcham and Richard Steiff
Telegraph, electric	1830	Samuel Morse
Telegraph, transatlantic	1866	William Thompson
Telephone	1876	Alexander Graham Bell
Telescope	1608	Hans Lippershey; perfected by Galileo Galilei in 1609
Telescope, reflecting	1672	Isaac Newton
Television	1926	Baird, Scotland; Jenkins, US; Mihaly, Germany
Theodolite	1787	Jesse Ramsden
Thermometer, mercury	1714	Gabriel Fahrenheit
Thimble	1684	Nicholas van Benschoten
Toaster, pop-up	1927	Charles Strite
Toilet, flush	1589	John Harington
Toothbrush	1498	China
Train, high-speed (TGV)	1978	France
Tram	1775	John Outram
Transistor	1947	Shockley, Bardeen, Brattain
Tuning fork	1711	John Shore
Tupperware	1945	Earl W Tupper
Typewriter	1808	Pelegrino Turri
Tyre, pneumatic	1888	John Boyd Dunlop
Vacuum cleaner	1869	Ives W McGaffey (also attrib. to H C Booth, 1901)
Vaseline	1879	Robert Cheseborough
Velcro	1948	George de Mestral
Vulcanized rubber	1839	Charles Goodyear
Walkman	1979	Sony
Washing machine, electric	1907	Hurley Machine Co
Waterproof material	1823	Charles Mackintosh
Windmill	644	Persia (Iran)
Wristwatch	1790	Droz and Leschot
Writing	c.3600–3500 BC	Sumerian civilization
X-rays	1895	Wilhelm von Röntgen
Zip fastener	1893	Whitcombe L Judson

E NUMBERS

An E number is a series of numbers prefixed by the letter E, indicating a food additive recognized by the European Union. Many of these appear on the packaging of processed food, and the following list identifies some of those more commonly found.

Number	Additive	Use
E100	curcumin	colorant
E101	riboflavin	colorant
E102	tartrazine	colorant
E104	quinoline	colorant
E150	caramel	colorant
E153	vegetable carbon	colorant
E162	betanin (beetroot red)	colorant
E170	calcium carbonate	various
E171	titanium oxide	colorant
E174	silver	colorant
E200	sorbic acid	preservative
E201	sodium sorbate	preservative
E202	potassium sorbate	preservative
E203	calcium sorbate	preservative
E210	benzoic acid	preservative
E221	sodium sulphite	preservative
E227	calcium bisulphite	preservative
E252	potassium nitrate	preservative
E260	acetic acid	various
E290	carbon dioxide	adds 'fizz' to drinks

Number	Additive	Use
E300	L-ascorbic acid	antioxidant
E307	synthetic alpha-tocopherol	antioxidant
E310	propyl gallate	antioxidant
E320	butylated hydroxytoluene	antioxidant
E322	lecithin	emulsifier/stabilizer
E330	citric acid	various
E334	tartaric acid	various
E338	orthophosphoric acid	flavouring
E400	alginic acid	emulsifier/stabilizer
E407	carrageenan	emulsifier/stabilizer
E410	carob gum	emulsifier/stabilizer
E412	guar gum	emulsifier/stabilizer
E413	gum tragacanth	emulsifier/stabilizer
E414	gum arabic	emulsifier/stabilizer
E420	sorbitol	sweetener
E440	pectin	emulsifier/stabilizer
E465	ethylmethylcellulose	emulsifier/stabilizer

Arts

POETS LAUREATE

In the 15th century Oxford and Cambridge universities gave the title 'laureate' to various poets. The title got its modern status in 1668 when John Dryden was given a stipend to write court poetry and celebrate state occasions in verse.

Name	Appointed
Samuel Daniel	1599
Ben Jonson	1616
Sir William d'Avenant	1638
John Dryden	1668
Thomas Shadwell	1689
Nathan Tate	1692
Nicholas Rowe	1715
Rev. Laurence Eusden	1718
Colley Cibber	1730
William Whitehead	1757
Thomas Warton	1785
Henry James Pye	1790
Robert Southey	1813
William Wordsworth	1843
Alfred Lord Tennyson	1850
Alfred Austin	1896

Name	Appointed
Robert Bridges	1913
John Masefield	1930
Cecil Day Lewis	1968
Sir John Betjeman	1972
Edward (Ted) Hughes	1984
Andrew Motion	1999

MAN BOOKER PRIZE

Established in 1969 by Booker McConnell engineering company for British, Irish and Commonwealth fiction.

Year	Title	Author
1969	*Something to Answer For*	P H Newby
1970	*The Elected Member*	Bernice Rubens
1971	*In a Free State*	V S Naipaul
1972	*G*	John Berger
1973	*The Siege of Krishnapur*	J G Farrell
1974	*The Conservationist*	Nadine Gordimer
	Holiday	Stanley Middleton
1975	*Heat and Dust*	Ruth Prawer Jhabvala
1976	*Saville*	David Storey
1977	*Staying On*	Paul Scott
1978	*The Sea, The Sea*	Iris Murdoch
1979	*Offshore*	Penelope Fitzgerald
1980	*Rites of Passage*	William Golding

Year	Title	Author
1981	*Midnight's Children*	Salman Rushdie
1982	*Schindler's Ark*	Thomas Keneally
1983	*Life and Times of Michael K*	J M Coetzee
1984	*Hotel du Lac*	Anita Brookner
1985	*The Bone People*	Keri Hulme
1986	*The Old Devils*	Kingsley Amis
1987	*Moon Tiger*	Penelope Lively
1988	*Oscar and Lucinda*	Peter Carey
1989	*The Remains of the Day*	Kazuo Ishiguro
1990	*Possession*	A S Byatt
1991	*The Famished Road*	Ben Okri
1992	*Sacred Hunger*	Barry Unsworth
	The English Patient	Michael Ondaatje
1993	*Paddy Clarke Ha Ha Ha*	Roddy Doyle
1994	*How Late It Was, How Late*	James Kelman
1995	*The Ghost Road*	Pat Barker
1996	*Last Orders*	Graham Swift
1997	*The God of Small Things*	Arundhati Roy
1998	*Amsterdam*	Ian McEwan
1999	*Disgrace*	J M Coetzee
2000	*The Blind Assassin*	Margaret Atwood
2001	*True History of the Kelly Gang*	Peter Carey
2002	*The Life of Pi*	Yann Martel
2003	*Vernon God Little*	DBC Pierre
2004	*The Line of Beauty*	Alan Hollinghurst

PULITZER PRIZE

US literature prize established in 1917 by Joseph Pulitzer.

Year	Title	Author
1981	*A Confederacy of Dunces*	John Kennedy Toole
1982	*Rabbit is Rich*	John Updike
1983	*The Color Purple*	Alice Walker
1984	*Ironweed*	William Kennedy
1985	*Foreign Affairs*	Alison Lurie
1986	*Lonesome Dove*	Larry McMurtry
1987	*A Summons to Memphis*	Peter Taylor
1988	*Beloved*	Toni Morrison
1989	*Breathing Lessons*	Anne Tyler
1990	*The Mambo Kings Play Songs of Love*	Oscar Hijuelos
1991	*Rabbit at Rest*	John Updike
1992	*A Thousand Acres*	Jane Smiley
1993	*A Good Scent from a Strange Mountain*	Robert Olen Butler
1994	*The Shipping News*	E Annie Proulx
1995	*The Stone Diaries*	Carol Shields
1996	*Independence Day*	Richard Ford
1997	*Martin Dressler: The Tale of An American Dreamer*	Steven Millhauser
1998	*American Pastoral*	Philip Roth
1999	*The Hours*	Michael Cunningham

Year	Title	Author
2000	*Interpreter of Maladies*	Jhumpa Lahiri
2001	*The Amazing Adventures of Kavalier & Clay*	Michael Chabon
2002	*Empire Falls*	Richard Russo
2003	*Middlesex*	Jeffrey Eugenides
2004	*The Known World*	Edward P Jones
2005	*Gilead*	Marilynne Robinson

PRIX GONCOURT

Annual Académie Goncourt prize for a French fiction work.

Year	Title	Author
1981	*Anne-Marie*	Lucien Bodard
1982	*Dans la main de l'ange*	Dominique Fernandez
1983	*Les égarés*	Frederick Tristan
1984	*L'amant*	Marguerite Duras
1985	*Les noces barbares*	Yann Queffelec
1986	*Valet de nuit*	Michel Host
1987	*La nuit sacrée*	Tahir Ben Jelloun
1988	*L'Exposition coloniale*	Erik Orsenna
1989	*Un grand pas vers le Bon Dieu*	Jean Vautrin
1990	*Les champs d'honneur*	Jean Rouault
1991	*Les filles du Calvaire*	Pierre Cambescot
1992	*Texaco*	Patrick Chamoiseau

Year	Title	Author
1993	*Le Rocher de Tanios*	Amin Maalouf
1994	*Un aller simple*	Didier van Cauwelaert
1995	*Le testament français*	Andrei Makine
1996	*Le chasseur Ó*	Pascale Roze
1997	*Le bataille*	Patrick Rambaud
1998	*Confidence pour confidence*	Paul Constant
1999	*Je m'en vais*	Jean Echenoz
2000	*Jean-Jacques Schuhl*	Ingrid Caven Gallimard
2001	*Rouge Bresil*	Jean-Christophe Rufin
2002	*Les Ombres Errantes*	Pascal Quignard
2003	*La Maîtresse de Brecht*	Jacques-Pierre Amette
2004	*Le Soleil des Scorta*	Laurent Gaudé

NOBEL PRIZE IN LITERATURE

1901	Rene Sully Prudhomme
1902	Theodor Mommsen
1903	Bjornestjerne Bjornson
1904	Frederic Mistral/ Juan Echegaray
1905	Henryk Sienkiewicz
1906	Giosue Carducci
1907	Rudyard Kipling
1908	Rudolf Eucken
1909	Selma Lagerlof
1910	Paul Von Heyse
1911	Maurice Maeterlinck
1912	Gerhart Hauptmann
1913	Sir Rabindranath Tagore
1914	*No award*
1915	Romain Rolland
1916	Verner Von Heidenstam
1917	Karl Gjellerup/Henrik Pontoppidan
1918	*No award*

1919 Carl Spitteler
1920 Knut Hamsun
1921 Anatole France
1922 Jacinto Benavente
1923 William Butler Yeats
1924 Wladyslaw Reymont
1925 George Bernard Shaw
1926 Grazia Deledda
1927 Henri Bergson
1928 Sigrid Undset
1929 Thomas Mann
1930 Sinclair Lewis
1931 Erik Karlfeldt
1932 John Galsworthy
1933 Ivan Bunin
1934 Luigi Pirandello
1935 *No award*
1936 Eugene O'Neill
1937 Roger Martin du Gard
1938 Pearl S Buck
1939 Frans Eemil Sillanpää
1940–43 *No award*
1944 Johannes V Jensen
1945 Gabriela Mistral
1946 Hermann Hesse
1947 André Gide
1948 Thomas Stearns Eliot
1949 William Faulkner
1950 Bertrand Russell
1951 Par Lagerkvist
1952 François Mauriac
1953 Sir Winston Churchill
1954 Ernest Hemingway
1955 Halidor Laxness
1956 Juan Ramón Jiménez
1957 Albert Camus
1958 Boris Pasternak (declined)
1959 Salvatore Quasimodo
1960 Saint-John Perse
1961 Ivo Andric
1962 John Steinbeck
1963 George Seferis
1964 Jean-Paul Sartre (declined)
1965 Mikhail Sholokhov
1966 Shmuel Yosef Agnonnelly Sachs
1967 Miguel Angel Asturias
1968 Yasunan Kawabata

1969 Samuel Beckett
1970 Alexander Solzhenitsyn
1971 Pablo Neruda
1972 Heinrich Böll
1973 Patrick White
1974 Eyvind Johnson/Harry Edmund Martinson
1975 Eugenio Montale
1976 Saul Bellow
1977 V Alexandre
1978 Isaac Bashevis Singer
1979 Odysseus Alepoudhelis
1980 Czeslaw Milosz
1981 Elias Canetti
1982 Gabriel Garcia Márquez
1983 William Gerald Golding
1984 Jaraslav Seifert
1985 Claude Simon
1986 Wole Soyinka
1987 Joseph Brodsky
1988 Naguib Mahfouz
1989 Camilo José Cela
1990 Octavio Paz
1991 Nadine Gordimer
1992 Derek Walcott
1993 Toni Morrison
1994 Kenzaburo Oe
1995 Seamus Heaney
1996 Wislawa Szymborska
1997 Dario Fo
1998 Jose Saramago
1999 Gunther Grass
2000 Gao Xingjian
2001 V S Naipaul
2002 Imre Kertész
2003 J M Coetzee
2004 Elfriede Jelinek

THE OSCARS

Year	Best film	Best actor
1927/8	*Wings*	Emil Jannings
1928/9	*Broadway Melody*	Warner Baxter
1929/30	*All Quiet on the Western Front*	George Arliss
1930/1	*Cimarron*	Lionel Barrymore
1931/2	*Grand Hotel*	Frederick March Wallace Beery
1932/3	*Cavalcade*	Charles Laughton
1934	*It Happened One Night*	Clark Gable
1935	*Mutiny on the Bounty*	Victor McLaglen
1936	*The Great Ziegfeld*	Paul Muni
1937	*The Life of Emile Zola*	Spencer Tracy
1938	*You Can't Take It With You*	Spencer Tracy
1939	*Gone with the Wind*	Robert Donat
1940	*Rebecca*	James Stewart
1941	*How Green Was My Valley*	Gary Cooper
1942	*Mrs Miniver*	James Cagney
1943	*Casablanca*	Paul Lukas
1944	*Going My Way*	Bing Crosby
1945	*The Lost Weekend*	Ray Milland
1946	*The Best Years of Our Lives*	Fredric March
1947	*Gentleman's Agreement*	Ronald Colman
1948	*Hamlet*	Laurence Olivier
1949	*All the King's Men*	Broderick Crawford
1950	*All About Eve*	José Ferrer
1951	*An American in Paris*	Humphrey Bogart
1952	*The Greatest Show on Earth*	Gary Cooper
1953	*From Here to Eternity*	William Holden
1954	*On the Waterfront*	Marlon Brando

Best actress

Janet Gaynor
Mary Pickford
Norma Shearer

Marie Dressler
Helen Hayes

Katharine Hepburn
Claudette Colbert
Bette Davis
Luise Rainer
Luise Rainer
Bette Davis
Vivien Leigh
Ginger Rogers
Joan Fontaine
Greer Garson
Jennifer Jones
Ingrid Bergman
Joan Crawford
Olivia de Havilland
Loretta Young
Jane Wyman
Olivia de Havilland
Judy Holliday
Vivien Leigh
Shirley Booth
Audrey Hepburn
Grace Kelly

Best director

Frank Borzage
Frank Lloyd
Lewis Milestone

Norman Taurog
Frank Borzage

Frank Lloyd
Frank Capra
John Ford
Frank Capra
Leo McCarey
Frank Capra
Victor Fleming
John Ford
John Ford
William Wyler
Michael Curtiz
Leo McCarey
Billy Wilder
William Wyler
Elia Kazan
John Huston
Joseph L Mankiewicz
Joseph L Mankiewicz
George Stevens
John Ford
Fred Zinnemann
Elia Kazan

Year	Best film	Best actor
1955	*Marty*	Ernest Borgnine
1956	*Around the World in Eighty Days*	Yul Brynner
1957	*The Bridge on the River Kwai*	Alec Guinness
1958	*Gigi*	David Niven
1959	*Ben-Hur*	Charlton Heston
1960	*The Apartment*	Burt Lancaster
1961	*West Side Story*	Maximilian Schell
1962	*Lawrence of Arabia*	Gregory Peck
1963	*Tom Jones*	Sidney Poitier
1964	*My Fair Lady*	Rex Harrison
1965	*The Sound of Music*	Lee Marvin
1966	*A Man for All Seasons*	Paul Scofield
1967	*In the Heat of the Night*	Rod Steiger
1968	*Oliver*	Cliff Robertson
1969	*Midnight Cowboy*	John Wayne
1970	*Patton*	George C Scott
1971	*The French Connection*	Gene Hackman
1972	*The Godfather*	Marlon Brando
1973	*The Sting*	Jack Lemmon
1974	*The Godfather Part II*	Art Carney
1975	*One Flew Over the Cuckoo's Nest*	Jack Nicholson
1976	*Rocky*	Peter Finch
1977	*Annie Hall*	Richard Dreyfuss
1978	*The Deer Hunter*	Jon Voight
1979	*Kramer vs Kramer*	Dustin Hoffman
1980	*Ordinary People*	Robert de Niro
1981	*Chariots of Fire*	Henry Fonda
1982	*Gandhi*	Ben Kingsley

Best actress

Anna Magnani
Ingrid Bergman

Joanne Woodward
Susan Hayward
Simone Signoret
Elizabeth Taylor
Sophia Loren
Anne Bancroft
Patricia Neal
Julie Andrews
Julie Christie
Elizabeth Taylor
Katharine Hepburn
Katharine Hepburn/
Barbra Streisand
Maggie Smith
Glenda Jackson
Jane Fonda
Liza Minnelli
Glenda Jackson
Ellen Burstyn
Louise Fletcher

Faye Dunaway
Diane Keaton
Jane Fonda
Sally Field
Sissy Spacek
Katharine Hepburn
Meryl Streep

Best director

Delbert Mann
George Stevens

David Lean
Vincente Minnelli
William Wyler
Billy Wilder
Robert Wise
David Lean
Tony Richardson
George Cukor
Robert Wise
Fred Zinnemann
Mike Nichols
Carole Reed

John Schlesinger
Franklin J Schaffner
William Friedkin
Bob Fosse
George Roy Hill
Francis Ford Coppola
Milos Forman

John G Avildsen
Woody Allen
Michael Cimino
Robert Benton
Robert Redford
Warren Beatty
Richard Attenborough

Year	Best film	Best actor
1983	*Terms of Endearment*	Robert Duvall
1984	*Amadeus*	F Murray Abraham
1985	*Out of Africa*	William Hurt
1986	*Platoon*	Paul Newman
1987	*The Last Emperor*	Michael Douglas
1988	*Rain Man*	Dustin Hoffman
1989	*Driving Miss Daisy*	Daniel Day Lewis
1990	*Dances with Wolves*	Jeremy Irons
1991	*Silence of the Lambs*	Anthony Hopkins
1992	*Unforgiven*	Al Pacino
1993	*Schindler's List*	Tom Hanks
1994	*Forest Gump*	Tom Hanks
1995	*Braveheart*	Nicholas Cage
1996	*The English Patient*	Geoffrey Rush
1997	*Titanic*	Jack Nicholson
1998	*Shakespeare in Love*	Roberto Benigni
1999	*American Beauty*	Kevin Spacey
2000	*Gladiator*	Russell Crowe
2001	*A Beautiful Mind*	Denzel Washington
2002	*Chicago*	Adrien Brody
2003	*The Lord of the Rings: The Fellowship of the Ring*	Johnny Depp
2004	*Million Dollar Baby*	Jamie Foxx

MUSICAL EXPRESSION AND TEMPO INSTRUCTIONS

Instruction	Meaning
accelerando	with increasing speed
adagio	slowly
agitato	in an agitated manner

Best actress	Best director
Shirley Maclaine	James L Brooks
Sally Field	Milos Forman
Geraldine Page	Sydney Pollack
Marlee Matlin	Oliver Stone
Cher	Bernardo Bertolucci
Jodie Foster	Barry Levinson
Jessica Tandy	Oliver Stone
Kathy Bates	Kevin Costner
Jodie Foster	Jonathan Demme
Emma Thompson	Clint Eastwood
Holly Hunter	Steven Spielberg
Jessica Lange	Robert Zemeckis
Susan Sarandon	Mel Gibson
Frances McDormand	Anthony Minghella
Helen Hunt	James Cameron
Gwyneth Paltrow	Steven Spielberg
Hilary Swank	Sam Mendes
Julia Roberts	Steven Soderbergh
Halle Berry	Ron Howard
Nicole Kidman	Roman Polanski
Charlize Theron	Peter Jackson
Hilary Swank	Clint Eastwood

Instruction	Meaning
allegretto	fairly quickly or briskly
allegro	quickly; in a brisk, lively manner
amoroso	lovingly

Instruction	Meaning
andante	at a moderately slow tempo
andantino	slightly faster than andante
animato	in a lively manner
appassionato	impassioned
assai	very
calando	with gradually decreasing tone and speed
cantabile	in a singing style
con	with
con affeto	with tender emotion
con amore	lovingly
con anima	with spirit
con brio	vigorously
con fuoco	with fire
con moto	quickly
crescendo	gradual increase in loudness
diminuendo	gradual decrease in loudness
dolce	gently and sweetly
doloroso	in a sorrowful manner
energico	energetically
espressivo	expressively
forte	loud; loudly
fortissimo	very loud
furioso	in a frantically rushing manner
giocoso	merry
grave	solemn and slow
grazioso	graceful
lacrimoso	sad and mournful
larghetto	slightly less slowly and broadly than largo
largo	slowly and broadly
legato	smoothly and connectedly
leggiero	light
lento	slowly
maestoso	majestically
marziale	martial

Instruction	Meaning
mezzo	moderately
moderato	at a moderate tempo
molto	very
non tanto	not too much
non troppo	not too much
pianissimo	very quietly
piano	softly
più	more
pizzicato	to be plucked with the finger
poco	a little
pomposo	in a pompous manner
prestissimo	even faster than presto
presto	very fast
quasi	almost; as if
rallentando	becoming slower
rubato	with a flexible tempo
scherzando	in jocular style
sciolto	free and easy
semplice	simple and unforced
sforzando	with strong initial attack
smorzando	dying away
sospirando	sighing; plaintive
sostenuto	in a smooth and sustained manner
sotto voce	extremely quiet
staccato	short, clipped and separate
strascinando	stretched out
strepitoso	noisy
stringendo	with increasing speed
tanto	too much
tardo	slow
troppo	too much
vivace	in a brisk, lively manner
volante	flying; fast and light

Languages

TYPOGRAPHIC, SCIENTIFIC AND MATHEMATICAL SYMBOLS

+	Addition	−	Subtraction
×	Multiplication	÷	Division
=	Equals	≠	Does not equal
≡	Identical; congruent	≈	Approximately equals
>	Greater than	<	Less than
≫	Much greater than	≪	Much less than
≯	Not greater than	≮	Not less than
≅	Isomorphic	:	Ratio
::	Used between ratios	∞	Infinity
∴	Therefore	∵	Since; because
⇒	Gives; leads on to	∠	Angle
∟	Right angle	⊥	Perpendicular
∇	Nablus	∂	Differential
δ	Delta	λ	Lambda
ε	Epsilon	ν	Nu
μ	Mu	≶	Greater or less than

|| Parallel

⌒ Arc

□ Square

▱ Parallelogram

Σ Sum

∪ Union

∈ Belongs to

{} Set braces

◁ Normal subgroup of

σ Standard deviation (population)

s Standard deviation (sample)

e Base of natural logarithms

∀ For all

Å Angstrom unit

Ω Ohm

p Radius of curvature

&c Etcetera

{} Braces

[] Square brackets

○ Circle

△ Triangle

▭ Rectangle

√ Square Root

∫ Integral

∩ Intersection

⊂ A subset of

ø Empty set absolute value

μ Mean (population)

× Mean (sample)

π Ratio of circumference of any circle to its diameter

iff If and only if

λ Wavelength

μ Magnetic permeability

h Planck constant

& Ampersand

< Derived from

() Parentheses

ACCENTS

Name	Character	Example	Name	Character	Example
Acute	´	é	Grave	`	è
Angstrom	°	å	Haček	ˇ	č
Breve	˘	ă	Macron	¯	ā
Cedilla	¸	ç	Tilde	~	ñ
Circumflex	^	î	Umlaut	¨	ü
Diaeresis	¨	ï			

THE APOSTROPHE

One of the most ill-used punctuation marks in the English language.

It is used:

1. To show the possessive case

a The apostrophe for this should only be used for proper and common nouns and not for the following pronouns: hers, its (it's = it is), ours, theirs, yours.

b In nouns (sing. and plural) that end in a letter other than *s*, the apostrophe must precede the added *s*, as in the chief's tent, men's boots, the fox's earth.

c In nouns (sing.) that end in *s*, the possessive is usually formed by adding the *'s*, as in the octopus's tentacles.

d In nouns (plural) that end in *s*, the apostrophe must follow the *s*, as in the boys' clothing, the octopuses' tentacles.

e When the added *s* is silent in speech it is usually omitted, as in for goodness' sake.

f In English names and surnames add *'s*, as in Burns's poems, St James's Road; but sound often demands the omission of another *s*, as in Bridges' poems.

g Ancient names ending in s usually omit a further *s*, as in Moses' law, Jesus' love.

h Abbreviations add *'s* when singular, as in the MP's constituency, and *s'* when plural, as in MPs' salaries.

2. To show omission

   Examples: e'er (ever), tho' (though), he's (he is, he has), it's (it is), '67 (1967 or contextual century)

don't (do not)	haven't (have not)	shan't (shall not)
shouldn't (should not)	won't (will not)	isn't (is not)
doesn't (does not)	daren't (dare not)	couldn't (could not)
can't (cannot)	mustn't (must not)	hasn't (has not)
there'll (there will)	I'll (I will)	we'll (we will)
you'll (you will)	who'll (who will)	they'll (they will)
I'd (I had, would)	who'd (who would)	I'm (I am)
you're (you are)	who's (who is, *not* pronoun, i.e. whose is that?)	

   But note: couldst canst shouldst wouldst

   These are the correct grammatical forms, not apostrophe-free abbreviations.

3. Irish names

   Example: O'Reilly.

AMERICAN SPELLING AND WORD VARIATIONS

British	American
aeroplane	airplane
aluminium	aluminum
armoury	armory
autumn	fall
bill	check
biscuit	cookie
braces	suspenders
bumbag	fannybag
calibre	caliber
callipers	calipers
callisthenics	calisthenics
car bonnet	hood
car boot	car trunk
car bumper	fender
caretaker	janitor
catalogue	catalog
centre	center
chemist	druggist, drugstore
cheque	check
colour	color
cosy	cozy
courgette	zucchini
crisps	(potato) chips
cupboard	closet
defence	defense
demagogue	demagog

British	American
dialling	dialing
dialogue	dialog
draughts (game)	checkers
dummy (baby)	pacifier
dustbin	garbage can, trashcan
endeavour	endeavor
enfold	infold
enrolled	enroled
epilogue	epilog
estate agent	real-estate agent, realtor
faeces	feces
favour	favor
fervour	fervor
fizzy drink	soda
flavour	flavor
foetus	fetus
gelatine	gelatin
glycerine	glycerin
grey	gray
grill	broil
gynaecology	gynecology
haemorrhage	hemorrhage
harbour	harbor
honour	honor

British	American
humour	humor
kerb	curb
ketchup	catchup
licence	license
lift	elevator
liquorice	licorice
manoeuvre	maneuver
meagre	meager
metre	meter
motorway	expressway, freeway
mould	mold
nappy	diaper
neighbour	neighbor
ochre	ocher
offence	offense
off-licence	liquor store
organdie	organdy
orthopaedic	orthopedic
paediatrics	pediatrics
paraffin	kerosene
pavement	sidewalk
pedlar	peddler
petrol	gas(oline)
plough	plow
postcode	zipcode
pretence	pretense
programme	program
pyjamas	pajamas
railway	railroad

British	American
rateable	ratable
reconnoitre	reconnoiter
restroom	lavatory
return ticket	round-trip ticket
rigour	rigor
saleable	salable
saloon	sedan
sanatorium	sanitarium
sceptic	skeptic
single ticket	one-way ticket
spring onion	scallion
stalls (theatre)	orchestra
sulphur	sulfur
sweets	candies
tap	faucet
theatre	theater
torch	flashlight
trainers	sneakers
tramp	hobo
traveller	traveler
trousers	pants
tumour	tumor
underpants	shorts
valour	valor
vest	undershirt
waistcoat	vest
wallet	billfold
whisky	whiskey

FIELDS OF STUDY

Name	Field of Study
Abiology	Inanimate objects
Acarology	Mites, ticks
Actinology	Chemical effects of light in certain wavelengths
Adenology	Glands
Aeroballistics	Science of ballistics as applied to aerodynamics
Aerodynamics	Motions of air and gases, especially in relation to moving objects
Aerography	Atmospheric conditions
Aerolithology	Meteors
Aerolitics	Aerolites (stormy meteors)
Aerology	Planet Mars
Aerometry	Properties of air
Aeronautics	Technology of flying aeroplanes
Aerophysics	Earth's atmosphere (especially effects of high-speed flying bodies)
Aerostatics	Construction/operation of lighter-than- air craft such as balloons
Aesthetics	Principles of beauty and the beautiful
Aetiology	Philosophy of causation
Agmatology	Bone fractures
Agriology	Comparative study of the customs of primitive peoples
Agrobiology	Soil management
Agrogeology	Adaptability of land to agriculture
Agrology	Crop production
Agronomy	Management in farming
Agrostology	Grasses (*also called* graminology)
Alethiology	Branch of logic concerned with truth and error

Name	Field of Study
Algebra	Branch of mathematics which uses letters and other symbols to represent numbers, values, etc.
Algology	Seaweeds and algae
Alimentology	Nutrition (*also called* trophology)
Allergology	Allergies
Ambrology	Sources/formation of amber
Ampelography	Grapes
Amphibiology	Amphibians
Anatomy	Human body and its parts
Anemology	Winds
Angiology	Blood vessels and lymphatic system
Anthoecology	Flowers and their environment
Anthropometry	Proportions, size and weight of human body
Anthropogeny	Human origins
Anthropogeography	Geographical distribution of mankind and its relationship with the environment
Anthropography	Geographical distribution of different races
Anthropology	Mankind, especially origins and customs
Anthroposociology	Sociology of race using anthropological methods
Antinology	Chemical effects of light in certain wavelengths
Apiology	Honey bees
Apologetics	Defences or proofs of Christianity
Arachnology	Spiders
Archaeogeology	Geological features of distant past
Archaeology	Human remains and artefacts
Architectonics	(1) Systematization of knowledge (2) Science of architecture
Archology	(1) Science of origins (2) Science of government
Areology	Planet Mars
Aretaics	Study of virtue

Name	Field of Study
Arthrology	Joints of the body
Assyriology	Ancient Assyria
Astrogation	Space navigation
Astrogeology	Geological features of celestial bodies, especially the moon and solar planets
Astrognosy	Fixed stars
Astrolithology	Meteorites (*also called* meteoritics)
Astronautics	Space travel
Astronomy	Celestial bodies
Astrophysics	Origins and physical nature of celestial bodies
Atmology	Water vapour
Audiology	Hearing (especially impaired)
Autecology	Ecology of an individual plant or species
Autoecology	Relation of organisms to their environment
Avigation	Aerial navigation
Avionics	Electrical/electronic equipment used in aviation
Axiology	Values (ethics, aesthetics, religion, etc.)
Azoology	Inanimate nature
Bacteriology	Bacteria
Ballistics	Projectiles and firearms
Batology	Brambles
Bibliography	History of books
Bibliology	Doctrines of Bible
Bibliotics	Analysis of handwriting, especially manuscripts
Bioastronautics	Effects of space travel, especially on human body
Biochemistry	Chemical processes in living organisms
Bioclimatology	Relationship between living creatures and atmospheric conditions
Biodynamics	Physiological processes of plants and animals
Bioecology	Interrelationship of plant and animal life in a shared environment

Name	Field of Study
Biogeography	Geographical distribution of plants and animals
Biolinguistics	Relationship between physiology and speech
Biology	All living organisms
Bionics	How living creatures perform tasks and how this knowledge can be applied to automated or computer-driven equipment
Bionomics	*See* ecology
Biophysiology	Growth, structure and physiology of organs
Biostatics	Relationship between structure and function of plants and animals
Biotechnology	*See* ergonomics
Botany	All plant life (*also called* phytology)
Bryology	Mosses and liverworts
Cacogenics	Factors that influence degeneration in offspring, especially with respect to different races
Cambistry	Commercial exchange, especially international money values
Cardioangiology	Heart and blood vessels
Cardiodynamics	Forces and movements of the heart
Cardiology	Heart and its functions
Caricology	Sedges
Carpology	Fruits and seeds
Cartography	Map-making
Casuistry	Relationship of general ethical principles to particular problems
Catoptrics	Light reflection
Cecidiology	Galls produced on trees by fungi, etc.
Cetology	Whales
Chemistry	Composition, properties and behaviour of substances
Chondrology	Cartilage

Name	Field of Study
Chorology	Migrations and distributions of organisms
Chrematistics	Wealth
Christology	Nature and attitudes of Christ
Chromatology	Colours
Chrysology	Production of wealth, especially related to precious metals
Cinematography	Art of making cinema films
Climatology	Climates
Cliometrics	Application of mathematical principles to the study of history
Coccidology	Coccidea family (scales, mealy bugs, etc.)
Codicology	Early manuscripts
Coleopterology	Beetles, weevils
Conchology	Mollusc shells (*also called* malacology)
Cosmology	(1) Overall structure of physical universe (astronomy) (2) Origin, structure and evolution of universe (philosophy)
Criminology	Crime and criminals
Crustaceology	Crustaceans
Crustalogy	Surface of earth or moon
Cryogenics	Low temperatures and their effects
Cryology	Snow, ice
Cryptography	Secret writing, codes
Ctetology	Origin and development of acquired characteristics
Cultural anthropology	Creative achievements of societies
Cybernetics	Comparative study of complex electronic machines and human nervous system
Cynology	Dogs
Cytochemistry	Chemistry of living cells

Name	Field of Study
Cytology	Cells
Cytotechnology	Human cells, especially to detect cancer
Dactylography	Fingerprints
Dactylology	Sign language using hands
Demography	Vital and social statistics of populations
Demology	Human activities and social environments
Demonology	Demons
Dendrochronology	Examination of annual growth rings in trees to determine age
Dendrology	Trees
Deontology	Ethics
Dermatology	Skin, skin diseases
Desmidiology	Microscopic, unicellular algae
Desmopathology	Diseases of ligaments and tendons
Diabology	The Devil
Diagnostics	Diagnosis of illness/diseases
Didactics	Art/science of teaching
Dioptrics	Light refraction
Diplomatology	Analysis of original texts or documents
Dipterology	Diptera family (flies, mosquitoes, gnats, etc.)
Ecclesiology	Church building and decoration
Eccrinology	Secretions and secretory glands
Echinology	Sea urchins
Ecology	Relationship of living organisms to their environment (*also called* bionomics)
Economics	Production and distribution of wealth
Egyptology	Ancient Egypt
Electrobiology	Electrical activity in organisms/effect of electricity on organisms
Emblematology	Interpretation of emblems
Emetology	Causes of vomiting

Name	Field of Study
Emmenology	Menstruation
Endocrinology	Endocrine glands
Enterology	Intestines
Entomology	Insects (*also called* insectology)
Enzymology	Fermentation and enzymes (*also called* zymology)
Epidemiology	Incidence, distribution, control and prevention of diseases
Epigraphy	Deciphering and interpreting ancient inscriptions
Epiphytology	Plant diseases
Epistemology	Human knowledge, especially methods and validity of
Epizoology	Incidence and spread of animal diseases
Eremology	Deserts
Ergology	Physical and mental effects of work
Ergonomics	Relationship of man to his working environment (*also called* biotechnology)
Eschatology	Death and final destiny
Ethics	Moral principles and right action
Ethnology	Origin and development of all races and their relationships with each other
Ethology	Animal behaviour in relation to the environment
Etiology	Causes of diseases and why they spread
Etruscology	Etruscan civilization
Etymology	Origin and history of words
Eugenics	Improvement of a breed or species through selective breeding
Euthenics	Improvement of a race or breed by controlling external influences such as environment
Exegetics	Interpretation of biblical literature
Exobiology	Life beyond earth's atmosphere
Faunology	*See* zoogeography

Name	Field of Study
Filicology	Ferns (*also called* pteridology)
Fluviology	Watercourses, rivers
Foetology	Foetuses
Fromology	Cheese
Gastrology	Stomach functions and diseases
Gemmology	Gemstones
Genecology	Animal species and their environments
Genesiology	Human reproduction
Genetics	Heredity
Geodynamics	Forces within the earth
Geognosy	Constituent parts of the earth
Geogony	Formation of the earth
Geology	The earth
Geometry	Properties and relationships of angles, points, lines, surfaces and solids
Geomorphology	Earth's surface
Geratology	Ageing
Geriatrics	Care of the aged
Gerodontics	Dental problems of the aged
Glaciology	Glaciers
Glottogony	Origin of language
Glottology	Science of linguistics
Gnoseology	Philosophy of knowledge
Graminology	*See* agrostology
Grammar	Formal structure of a language
Graphology	Analysis of handwriting
Gynaecology	Disorders of the female reproductive system
Gyniatrics	Women's diseases
Gyrostatics	Rotating solid bodies
Haematology	Blood, diseases of the blood and blood-forming tissues

Name	Field of Study
Hagiography	Lives of the saints
Halology	Salts
Hamartiology	Doctrine of sin
Helcology	Ulcers
Helminthology	Worms (especially internal worms)
Hemipterology	Hemiptera family (bedbugs, aphids, etc.)
Heparology, hepatology	The liver
Heraldry	Genealogy (especially aristocratic lineage)
Hermeneutics	Interpretation and explanation (especially interpretation of the Bible)
Herniology	Hernias
Herpetology	Reptiles and amphibians
Heterology	Abnormalities of tissue structure
Hippiatrics	Horse diseases (*also called* hippopathology)
Hippology	Horses
Hippopathology	*See* hippiatrics
Histology	Microscopic features of animal and plant tissues
History	Past events, especially human affairs
Horometry	Measuring time
Horticulture	Cultivation of gardens
Hydraulics	Engineering applications of laws applying to water and other liquids in motion
Hydrodynamics	Forces acting on or produced by liquids (*also called* hydromechanics)
Hydrogeology	Water on/below the earth's surface
Hydrokinetics	Laws of gases/liquids in motion
Hydrology	Water on the earth and in the atmosphere
Hydromechanics	*See* hydrodynamics
Hydroponics	Growing plants in special solutions instead of soil
Hydrostatics	Equilibrium and pressure of liquids

Name	Field of Study
Hyetography	Geographical distribution of rainfall
Hygienics	Health and hygiene
Hygrology	Atmospheric humidity
Hymenopterology	Hymenoptera family (bees, wasps, ants, etc.)
Hypnology	Sleep, hypnotism
Hypsography	Land areas above sea level
Hysterology	The uterus
Iamatology	Remedies
Iatrochemistry	Application of chemistry for healing purposes
Ichnology	Fossil footprints
Ichthyology	Fish
Immunogenetics	Immunity with respect to genetic formation
Immunology	Immunity from disease
Insectology	*See* entomology
Isagogics	Biblical writings, emphasizing the literature and cultural history of the Bible
Kinematics	Motion of objects without reference to the external forces which cause the motion
Kinesics	'Body language' or non-verbal gestures of communication (*also called* pasimology)
Kinetics	Motion of objects with reference to the external forces acting on them
Koniology	Atmospheric dust and other airborne pollutants
Lalopathology	Speech disorders
Laryngology	Larynx
Lepidopterology	Butterflies and moths
Lexicology	The form, development and meaning of words
Lichenology	Lichens
Limnology	Ponds, lakes
Linguistics	Language and its structure
Lithology	Mineral composition and structure of rocks

Name	Field of Study
Liturgiology	Church rituals and their symbolism
Logistics	Movement and supply of troops
Macrobiotics	Longevity
Malacology	*See* conchology
Mammalogy	Mammals
Mathematics	Abstract study of number, quantity and space
Mensuration	Science of measurement
Merology	Body fluids and basic tissues
Metaethics	Foundation of ethics
Metalinguistics	Language in its cultural context
Metallurgy	Science of producing, refining and use of metals
Metamathematics	Logical analysis of basic principles of mathematics
Metaphysics	Theoretical study of being and knowing
Meteoritics	*See* astrolithology
Meteorology	Climate and weather variations
Methodology	(1) Application of reason to science and philosophy (2) The science of method (order) and classification
Metoposcopy	*See* physiognomy
Metrology	Science of weights and measures
Miasmology	Fogs, smogs
Microbiology	Micro-organisms
Micrology	Microscopic objects
Mineralogy	Minerals (*also called* oryctology)
Momiology	Mummies
Morphology	(1) Form and structure of animals and plants (2) Word formation patterns
Morphonomy	Laws of form in nature
Muscology	Mosses
Mycology	Fungi
Myology	Muscles, musculature
Myrmecology	Ants

Name	Field of Study
Nealogy	Early stages of animal development
Neonatology	The newborn
Neontology	Recently living plants and animals
Neossology	Young birds
Nephology	Clouds
Nephrology	Kidneys
Neurology	Nerves and nerve systems (especially diseases of)
Neuropsychiatry	Diseases of the mind and nervous system
Neuropterology	Neuroptera family (lacewings, etc.)
Nidology	Birds' nests
Noology	Intuition and reason
Obstetrics	Care of women before, during and after childbirth
Oceanography	Oceans, seas
Odontology	Teeth and surrounding tissues
Oenology	Making wines (*also called* viticulture)
Olfactology	Scientific study of the sense of smell
Ombrology	Rainfall
Oncology	Tumours
Oneirology	Science and interpretation of dreams
Onomastics	Names and their origins
Oology	Birds' eggs
Ophiology	Snakes
Ophthalmology	Eyes, eye diseases and defects
Optics	Properties of light (*also called* photology)
Organology	Organs of plants and animals
Ornithology	Birds
Orology	Scientific study of mountains
Orthodontics	Malformed teeth and other oral problems
Orthoepy	Correct pronunciation
Orthography	Correct spelling
Orthology	Correct use of language

Name	Field of Study
Orthopaedics	Bone and muscle deformities
Orthopsychiatry	Prevention of mental/behavioural disorders
Orthopterology	Orthoptera family (cockroaches, grasshoppers, etc.)
Orthoptics	Eye irregularities, especially muscle problems
Oryctology	*See* mineralogy
Osmonosology	Disorders of the sense of smell
Osteology	Bones and diseases of
Otolaryngology	Ear, nose and throat
Otology	Diseases of the ear
Ovology	Formation and structure of animal ova
Paedeutics	Science of learning
Paediatrics	Medical care of infants, children and adolescents
Paedogogics	Science or art of teaching/education
Palaeobiology	Fossil plants and animals
Palaeobotany	Fossil plants
Palaeoecology	Plants, animals and their environment in the distant past
Palaeoethnology	Early man
Palaeogeography	Features of the earth as they existed in past geological ages
Palaeography	Ancient writings
Palaeoichthyology	Fossil fish
Palaeology	Antiquities
Palaeomammalogy	Mammals of past ages
Palaeontology	Life in the geological past
Palaeopedology	Soils of past geological ages
Palaeopathology	Diseases from the distant past
Palaeornithology	Fossil birds
Palaeozoology	Fossil animals
Pantology	Systematic survey of all branches of learning
Parapsychology	Psychic phenomena

Name	Field of Study
Paroemiology	Proverbs
Pasimology	*See* kinesics
Pathognomy	The emotions and signs or expressions of emotion
Pathology	Causes, origin and nature of disease
Pedodontics	Children's dental care
Pedology	(1) Soils (2) Physical and psychological events of childhood
Pelycology	Pelvic structure
Penology	(1) Science of the punishment of crime (2) Science of the management of prisons
Perastadics	Space flying
Periodontics	Diseases of bone, tissue and gum (mouth)
Petrogenesis	Formation of rocks
Petrology	Origin, structure and composition of rocks
Phaenology	Climate and its effects on living organisms
Pharmacology	Preparation, use, effects and dosage of drugs
Pharyngology	Pharynx
Phenology	Organisms as affected by climate (e.g. migration of birds, blooming of flowers)
Philology	Science of language
Philosophy	Enquiry into truths and knowledge of reality
Phletology	Veins of the body
Phonetics	Vocal sounds (and their classification)
Phorology	Disease carriers, epidemics and endemic diseases
Photics	Light
Photodynamics	Light in relation to the movement of plants
Photology	*See* optics
Phyllotaxy	Arrangement and distribution of leaves
Physics	Interactions of matter and energy
Physiognomy	Determining aspects of character from physical, especially facial, features (*also called* metoposcopy)

Name	Field of Study
Physiography	Physical geography
Physiology	Functions of organisms and their parts
Phytobiology	Plant biology
Phytogeography	Geographical distribution of plants
Phytology	*See* botany
Pistology	Characteristics of faith
Pneumology	Human respiratory system
Polemics	History of ecclesiastical disputes
Pomology	Fruit
Ponerology	Sin, evil and wrong-doing
Potamology	Rivers
Praxeology	Human behaviour and conduct
Proctology	Disorders of rectum and anus
Protozoology	Protozoa (minute invertebrates, e.g. amoeba)
Psephology	Elections
Psychiatry	Study, treatment and prevention of mental illness
Psychodiagnostics	Evaluation of personality
Psycholinguistics	Relationship between language and behaviour patterns
Psychology	The mind and mental processes, emotions and desires
Psychopathology	Causes and nature of mental illness
Psychopharmacology	Drugs that alter emotional and mental conditions
Psychotherapy	Treating psychological disorders using psychological methods
Pteridology	*See* filicology
Pyretology	Fevers
Pyrology	Fire and heat, especially chemical analysis of
Radiogenetics	Effects of radioactivity on genes
Radiology	Radiation for diagnosis and therapy
Rhinology	The nose and its diseases

Name	Field of Study
Robotics	Application of automated machinery to accomplish tasks normally done by hand
Seismography	Measurement of earthquakes
Selenology	Moon
Semantics	Meaning of words (*also called* semasiology, sematology, semology)
Semiotics	Signs
Semitics	Semitic languages and culture
Serology	Serums
Siagonology	Jaw bones
Sindology	Funeral shrouds
Sinology	Chinese culture
Sociology	Origin, development, structure and function of human society
Somatology	Man's physical characteristics
Sophiology	Science of ideas
Speleology	Caves
Sphagnology	Sphagnum mosses
Sphygmology	The pulse
Splanchnology	Viscera (large internal organs of the body)
Spongology	Sponges
Statics	Matter and forces at rest or in equilibrium
Stirpiculture	Selective breeding
Stomatology	Diseases of the mouth
Stratigraphy	Stratified rocks
Sumerology	Sumerian civilization
Syndesmology	Ligaments of the body
Synecology	Relationships of various groups of organisms to a common environment
Syntax	Principles of grammatical sentence construction
Taxonomy	Principles of classification

Name	Field of Study
Tectonics	The earth's crust
Teleology	Ends or final causes with particular reference to evidence of purpose or design in nature
Telmatology	Wetlands, marshes, swamps
Tenology	Tendons
Teratology	Malfunctions in animals and plants
Testaceology	Shell-bearing animals
Thalassography	Areas of water such as gulfs, sounds, etc.
Thanatology	Death and the dead
Thaumatology	Miracles
Theology	Theistic religions (especially Christianity)
Theoretics	Theories and hypotheses (applied to any field of learning)
Thermodynamics	Relationship between heat and other types of energy
Thermogeography	Geographical factors affecting temperature
Thermokinematics	Movement of heat
Thermostatics	Equilibrium of heat
Thremmatology	Breeding of domestic plants and animals
Topology	(1) Characteristics of geometrical figures that remain unaffected by changes in shape or size (2) Plant localities
Toponymy	Place-names of a district
Toxicology	Poisons
Traumatology	Wounds and their treatment
Trichology	Hair and hair diseases
Trigonometry	Relationships of sides and angles of triangles
Trophology	*See* alimentology
Typhlology	Blindness and its prevention
Uranography	Studying and mapping the heavens
Urbanology	Urban problems and conditions

Name	Field of Study
Uredinology	Branch of mycology which studies rusts
Urology	Diseases of the kidney
Venereology	Venereal diseases
Vexillology	Flags, flag design
Virology	Viruses
Viticulture	*See* oenology
Volcanology	Volcanoes
Xylology	Structure of wood
Zenography	Jupiter (planet)
Zoobiology	*See* zoology
Zoogeography	Geographical distribution of animal life (also called faunology)
Zoology	All living creatures (*also called* zoobiology)
Zoopathology	Animal diseases
Zoophysiology	Animal physiology
Zoophytology	Zoophytes (animals such as sponges, corals, etc.)
Zoopsychology	Animal behaviour
Zymology	*See* enzymology

COLLECTIVE NOUNS

Noun	Collective term
actors	company
aldermen	bench, guzzle
antelopes	herd
apes	shrewdness
asses	pace, herd
badgers	cete
bakers	tabernacle
bears	sloth
bees	swarm, grist
birds	flock, congregation, flight, volery
bishops	bench
bitterns	sedge, siege
boars	sounder
bucks	brace, lease

Noun	Collective term
buffaloes	herd
bullfinches	bellowing
capercailzies	tok
cats	clowder
cattle	herd, drove
chickens	brood
choughs	chattering
colts	rag
coots	covert
cranes	herd, sedge, siege
critics	shrivel
crocodiles	bask
crows	murder
cubs	litter
curlews	herd
curs	cowardice
deer	herd
directors	board
dolphins	school
doves	flight, dule
ducks	paddling, team
dunlins	flight
eggs	clutch
elk	gang
fish	catch, shoal, run, draught, haul
flies	swarm, grist
flowers	bouquet
foxes	skulk
geese	gaggle, skein, flock

Noun	Collective term
giraffes	herd
gnats	swarm, cloud
goats	herd, tribe
goldfinches	charm
grouse	brood, covey, pack
gulls	colony
hares	down, husk
hawks	cast
hens	brood
herons	sedge, siege
herrings	shoal, glean
horses	herd, drove
hounds	pack, mute, cry
insects	swarm
inventions	budget
jellyfish	stuck, smuth
judges	bench
kangaroos	troop
kittens	kindle
lapwings	desert
larks	exaltation
leopards	leap
lions	pride, troop
magpies	tiding
mallards	sord, sute
mares	stud
martens	richesse
moles	labour
monkeys	troop
mules	barren
nightingales	watch
owls	parliament

Noun	Collective term
oxen	yoke, drove, team, herd
partridges	covey
peacocks	muster
people	audience, crowd, congregation, mob
pheasants	nye, nide
pigeons	flock, flight
pigs	litter
plovers	stand, wing
pochards	flight, rush, bunch, knob
policemen	posse
ponies	herd
porpoises	school, gam
poultry	run
prisoners	gang
pups	litter
quails	bevy
quotations	mellificium, rosary
rabbits	nest
racehorses	field, string
ravens	unkindness
remedies	rabble
roes	bevy
rooks	building, clamour
ruffs	hill
rumours	nest
sailors	crew
seals	herd, pod, rookery
sheep	flock
sheldrakes	dopping
ships	fleet
snipe	walk, wisp
sparrows	host
starlings	murmuration
stories	anthology
swallows	flight
swans	herd, bevy
swifts	flock
swine	herd, sounder, dryft
teal	bunch, knob, spring
thieves	gang
whales	school, gam, run, pod
whelps	litter
whiting	pod
wigeon	bunch, company, knob, flight
wildfowl	plump, sord, sute
wolves	pack, rout, herd
woodcocks	fall
workmen	gang

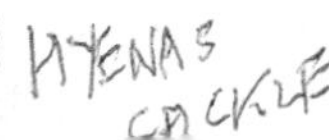

ANIMALS AND RELATED TERMS

Animal	Male	Female
ant		
ass	jack	jenny
badger		
bear		
bee		
bird	cock	hen
bull		
cat	tom	tabby
cod		
crab	cock	hen
crow		
deer	stag, hart	doe, hind
dog	dog	bitch
dove		
duck	drake	
eagle		
eel		
elephant	bull	cow
falcon	tercel, tiercel	
ferret	hob	gill, jill
fish		
fowl	cock	hen
fox	dog	vixen
frog		
goat	billy, buck	nanny
goose	gander	

Young	Habitation	Related adjective
	anthill, formicary	formic
		asinine
	sett	
cub		ursine
	apiary, hive	apian
chick, nestling, fledgling	nest	avian, ornithic
		taurine
kitten		feline
codling		
		cancroid
		corvine
fawn		cervine
pup, puppy		canine
		columbine
duckling		
eaglet	aerie, eyrie	aquiline
elver, grig		
calf		elephantine
eyas		falconine
kit		
fry, fingerling	redd	piscine, ichthyoid
		gallinaceous
kit, cub	earth	vulpine
tadpole		
kid, yeanling		caprine, hircine
gosling		anserine, anserous

Animal	Male	Female
gull		
hare	buck	doe
hawk		
herring		
horse	stallion	mare
kangaroo	buck, old man	
lion	lion	lioness
lobster	cock	hen
lynx		
mite, tick		
monkey		
otter	dog	
owl		
ox	bull	cow
parrot		
peafowl	peacock	peahen
pig	boar	sow
pigeon		
puffin		
rabbit	buck	doe
reindeer	buck	
rook		
ruff	ruff	reeve
salmon	cock	hen
seal		
sheep	ram, tup	ewe
snake		

Young	Habitation	Related adjective
		larine
leveret		leporine
		accipitrine
alevin, brit, sparling		
foal, colt, filly		equine
joey		
cub		leonine
		lyncean
		acaroid
		simian
	holt	
owlet		
calf		bovine
		psittacine
		pavonine
piglet	sty	porcine
squab		
	puffinry	alcidine
	warren	
	rookery	
alevin, grilse, parr, smolt		
pup	sealery	phocine
lamb, yeanling		ovine
		serpentine, anguine, ophidian, colubrine

Animal	Male	Female
squirrel		
swallow		
swan	cob	pen
termite		
tiger	tiger	tigress
wasp		
weasel	whittret	
whale	bull	cow
wolf		
wren		jenny

ENTHUSIASTS AND COLLECTORS

Area of interest	Term for enthusiast/collector
animals	zoophile
archery	toxophilite
bell-ringing	campanologist
books	bibliophile
cars	automobilist
cats	ailurophile
cigarette cards	cartophilist
coins	numismatist
crosswords	cruciverbalist

Young	Habitation	Related adjective
	drey, dray	
		hirundine
cygnet		
	termitarium	
cub		
	bike, vespiary	vespine
calf		
cub, whelp		lupine

Area of interest	Term for enthusiast/collector
flags	vexillologist
matchbox labels	phillumenist
phonecards	fusilatelist
postcards	deltiologist
share certificates	scripophile
stamps	philatelist
teddy bears	arctophile
umbrellas	brolliologist
wine	oenophile

-ARCHIES AND -OCRACIES

The suffixes -archy and -ocracy mean 'government by'. Therefore, in the following list hierocracy means 'government by priests' and triarchy means 'government by three people'.

Anarchy	Without law
Aristocracy	Privileged order
Autocracy	One man absolute rule
Bureaucracy	Officials
Democracy	The people
Despotocracy	A tyrant
Diarchy	Two rulers
Ergatocracy	The workers
Ethnocracy	Race or ethnic group
Gerontocracy	Old men
Gynarchy	Women
Gynaecocracy	Women
Gynocracy	Women
Hierocracy	Priests
Isocracy	All with equal power
Kakistocracy	The worst
Matriarchy	A mother (or mothers)
Meritocracy	In power on ability
Mobocracy	A mob
Monarchy	Hereditary head of state
Monocracy	One person
Ochlocracy	The mob
Oligarchy	Small exclusive class

Pantisocracy	All with equal power
Patriarchy	Male head of family
Plutocracy	The wealthy
Stratocracy	The military
Technocracy	Technical experts
Thearchy	God or gods
Theocracy	Divine guidance
Triarchy	Three people

INTERNATIONAL COMMUNICATION ALPHABET

Alpha	A	November	N
Bravo	B	Oscar	O
Charlie	C	Papa	P
Delta	D	Quebec	Q
Echo	E	Romeo	R
Foxtrot	F	Sierra	S
Golf	G	Tango	T
Hotel	H	Uniform	U
India	I	Victor	V
Juliet	J	Whiskey	W
Kilo	K	Xray	X
Lima	L	Yankee	Y
Mike	M	Zulu	Z

COMMON ACRONYMS

An acronym (literally, short name) differs from a standard abbreviation in that it is pronounceable as a word rather than a list of letters.

Acronym	Full form
ABTA	Association of British Travel Agents
ACAS	Advisory, Conciliation and Arbitration Service
Aids	Acquired Immune (or Immuno-) Deficiency Syndrome
ANZUS	Australia, New Zealand and US defence pact
AWOL	Absent Without Official Leave
BALPA	British Airline Pilots's Association
BUPA	British United Provident Association
CARICOM	Caribbean Community and Common Market
CAT (as in CAT scan)	Computerized Axial Tomography
COSLA	Convention of Scottish Local Authorities
DINKY	Double Income, No Kids Yet
ECHO virus	Enteric Cytopathic Human Orphan virus
EPOS	Electronic Point Of Sale
Ernie	Electronic Random Number Indicator Equipment

Acronym	Full form
FIFA	Fédération Internationale de Football Association
FIFO	First In, First Out
GATT	General Agreement on Tariffs and Trade
GIGO	Garbage In, Garbage Out
ISA	Individual Savings Account
laser	Light Amplification by Stimulated Emission of Radiation
MAFF	Ministry of Agriculture, Fisheries and Food
maser	Microwave Amplification by Stimulated Emission of Radiation
MASH	Mobile Army Surgical Hospital
Miras	Mortgage Interest Relief At Source
MIRV	Multiple Independently targeted Re-entry Vehicle
MORI	Market and Opinion Research International
NALGO	National And Local Government Officers' Association
Nato or NATO	North Atlantic Treaty Organization
NICAM	Near-Instantaneous Companding Audio Multiplex
NIMBY	Not In My Back Yard

Acronym	Full form
NIREX	Nuclear Industry Radioactive Waste Disposal Executive
Ofgas	Office of Gas Supply
Ofsted	Office for Standards in Education
Oftel	Office of Telecommunications
Ofwat	Office of Water Services
OPEC	Organization of Petroleum Exporting Countries
Oxfam	Oxford Committee for Famine Relief
QANTAS	Queensland And Northern Territory Aerial Service
quango	Quasi-Autonomous Non-Governmental Organization
RADA	Royal Academy of Dramatic Art
radar	Radio Detecting And Ranging
REME	Royal Electrical and Mechanical Engineers
SALT	Strategic Arms Limitation Talks (or Treaty)
SAM	Surface-to-Air Missile
SARS	Severe Acute Respiratory Syndrome
scuba	Self-Contained Underwater Breathing Apparatus
SERPS	State Earning-Related Pension Scheme
SIDS	Sudden Infant Death Syndrome
sonar	Sound Navigation And Ranging

Acronym	Full form
SWALK	Sealed With A Loving Kiss
SWAT	Special Weapons And Tactics
SWOT	Strengths, Weaknesses, Opportunities, Threats
Tardis	Time And Relative Dimension in Space
TEFL	Teaching of English as a Foreign Language
Tessa	Tax Exempt Special Savings Account
TWOC	Taking Without Owner's Consent
UCAS	Universities and Colleges Admissions Service
UEFA	Union of European Football Associations
UNESCO	United Nations Educational, Scientific and Cultural Organization
UNICEF	United Nations Children's Fund (formerly United Nations International Children's Emergency Fund)
VAT or Vat	Value-Added Tax
WASP	White Anglo-Saxon Protestant
wysiwyg	What You See Is What You Get
zip (as in zip code)	Zone Improvement Plan

Sport

AMERICAN FOOTBALL

The Super Bowl

End-of-season championship game between the respective winners of the American and National Football Conferences to determine the undisputed champions of the National Football League. First held in 1967 (Super Bowl I). All previous winners listed.

I	Green Bay Packers	XXII	Washington Redskins
II	Green Bay Packers	XXIII	San Francisco 49ers
III	New York Jets	XXIV	San Francisco 49ers
IV	Kansas City Chiefs	XXV	New York Giants
V	Baltimore Colts	XXVI	Washington Redskins
VI	Dallas Cowboys	XXVII	Dallas Cowboys
VII	Miami Dolphins	XXVIII	Dallas Cowboys
VIII	Miami Dolphins	XXIX	San Francisco 49ers
IX	Pittsburgh Steelers	XXX	Dallas Cowboys
X	Pittsburgh Steelers	XXXI	Green Bay Packers
XI	Oakland Raiders	XXXII	Denver Broncos
XII	Dallas Cowboys	XXXIII	Denver Broncos
XIII	Pittsburgh Steelers	XXXIV	St Louis Rams
XIV	Pittsburgh Steelers	XXXV	Baltimore Ravens
XV	Oakland Raiders	XXXVI	New England Patriots
XVI	San Francisco 49ers	XXXVII	Tampa Bay Buccaneers
XVII	Washington Redskins	XXXVIII	New England Patriots
XVIII	Los Angeles Raiders	XXXIX	New England Patriots
XIX	San Francisco 49ers		
XX	Chicago Bears		
XXI	New York Giants		

ASSOCIATION FOOTBALL

English Premier League Championship

The oldest league in world football. Founded in season 1888/89 and first won by Preston North End. Previous winners from 1949 (Season 1948/49). Known as the English First Division prior to 1993.

1949	Portsmouth	1971	Arsenal
1950	Portsmouth	1972	Derby County
1951	Tottenham Hotspur	1973	Liverpool
1952	Manchester Utd	1974	Leeds Utd
1953	Arsenal	1975	Derby County
1954	Wolverhampton W	1976	Liverpool
1955	Chelsea	1977	Liverpool
1956	Manchester Utd	1978	Nottingham Forest
1957	Manchester Utd	1979	Liverpool
1958	Wolverhampton W	1980	Liverpool
1959	Wolverhampton W	1981	Aston Villa
1960	Burnley	1982	Liverpool
1961	Tottenham Hotspur	1983	Liverpool
1962	Ipswich Town	1984	Liverpool
1963	Everton	1985	Everton
1964	Liverpool	1986	Liverpool
1965	Manchester Utd	1987	Everton
1966	Liverpool	1988	Liverpool
1967	Manchester Utd	1989	Arsenal
1968	Manchester City	1990	Liverpool
1969	Leeds Utd	1991	Arsenal
1970	Everton	1992	Leeds Utd

1993	Manchester Utd	2000	Manchester Utd
1994	Manchester Utd	2001	Manchester Utd
1995	Blackburn Rovers	2002	Arsenal
1996	Manchester Utd	2003	Manchester United
1997	Manchester Utd	2004	Arsenal
1998	Arsenal	2005	Chelsea
1999	Manchester Utd		

English FA Challenge Cup

The oldest and arguably the hardest tournament to win in world club football. Founded in season 1871/72 and first won by The Wanderers. Previous winners from 1949 (Season 1948/49).

1949	Wolverhampton W	1964	West Ham Utd
1950	Arsenal	1965	Liverpool
1951	Newcastle Utd	1966	Everton
1952	Newcastle Utd	1967	Tottenham Hotspur
1953	Blackpool	1968	West Bromwich A
1954	West Bromwich A	1969	Manchester City
1955	Newcastle Utd	1970	Chelsea
1956	Manchester City	1971	Arsenal
1957	Aston Villa	1972	Leeds Utd
1958	Bolton Wanderers	1973	Sunderland
1959	Nottingham Forest	1974	Liverpool
1960	Wolverhampton W	1975	West Ham Utd
1961	Tottenham Hotspur	1976	Southampton
1962	Tottenham Hotspur	1977	Manchester Utd
1963	Manchester Utd	1978	Ipswich Town

1979	Arsenal	1993	Arsenal
1980	West Ham Utd	1994	Manchester Utd
1981	Tottenham Hotspur	1995	Everton
1982	Tottenham Hotspur	1996	Manchester Utd
1983	Manchester Utd	1997	Chelsea
1984	Everton	1998	Arsenal
1985	Manchester Utd	1999	Manchester Utd
1986	Liverpool	2000	Chelsea
1987	Coventry City	2001	Liverpool
1988	Wimbledon	2002	Arsenal
1989	Liverpool	2003	Arsenal
1990	Manchester Utd	2004	Manchester United
1991	Tottenham Hotspur	2005	Arsenal
1992	Liverpool		

Scottish Premier League Championship

Founded in season 1890/91 and dominated throughout its rich history by the Glasgow giants Celtic and Rangers. Previous winners from 1949 (Season 1948/49). Known as the Scottish First Division prior to 1976.

1949	Glasgow Rangers	1957	Glasgow Rangers
1950	Glasgow Rangers	1958	Heart Of Midlothian
1951	Hibernian	1959	Glasgow Rangers
1952	Hibernian	1960	Heart Of Midlothian
1953	Glasgow Rangers	1961	Glasgow Rangers
1954	Glasgow Celtic	1962	Dundee
1955	Aberdeen	1963	Glasgow Rangers
1956	Glasgow Rangers	1964	Glasgow Rangers

1965	Kilmarnock	1986	Glasgow Celtic
1966	Glasgow Celtic	1987	Glasgow Rangers
1967	Glasgow Celtic	1988	Glasgow Celtic
1968	Glasgow Celtic	1989	Glasgow Rangers
1969	Glasgow Celtic	1990	Glasgow Rangers
1970	Glasgow Celtic	1991	Glasgow Rangers
1971	Glasgow Celtic	1992	Glasgow Rangers
1972	Glasgow Celtic	1993	Glasgow Rangers
1973	Glasgow Celtic	1994	Glasgow Rangers
1974	Glasgow Celtic	1995	Glasgow Rangers
1975	Glasgow Rangers	1996	Glasgow Rangers
1976	Glasgow Rangers	1997	Glasgow Rangers
1977	Glasgow Celtic	1998	Glasgow Celtic
1978	Glasgow Rangers	1999	Glasgow Rangers
1979	Glasgow Celtic	2000	Glasgow Rangers
1980	Aberdeen	2001	Glasgow Celtic
1981	Glasgow Celtic	2002	Glasgow Celtic
1982	Glasgow Celtic	2003	Glasgow Rangers
1983	Dundee Utd	2004	Glasgow Celtic
1984	Aberdeen	2005	Glasgow Rangers
1985	Aberdeen		

Scottish FA Challenge Cup

Following the great success of the English FA Challenge Cup a similar event was established north of the border in season 1873/74 and first won by Queens Park. Previous winners from 1949 (Season 1948/49).

1949	Glasgow Rangers	1951	Glasgow Celtic
1950	Glasgow Rangers	1952	Motherwell

1953	Glasgow Rangers	1980	Glasgow Celtic
1954	Glasgow Celtic	1981	Glasgow Rangers
1955	Clyde	1982	Aberdeen
1956	Heart Of Midlothian	1983	Aberdeen
1957	Falkirk	1984	Aberdeen
1958	Clyde	1985	Glasgow Celtic
1959	St Mirren	1986	Aberdeen
1960	Glasgow Rangers	1987	St Mirren
1961	Dunfermline Athletic	1988	Glasgow Celtic
1962	Glasgow Rangers	1989	Glasgow Celtic
1963	Glasgow Rangers	1990	Aberdeen
1964	Glasgow Rangers	1991	Motherwell
1965	Glasgow Celtic	1992	Glasgow Rangers
1966	Glasgow Rangers	1993	Glasgow Rangers
1967	Glasgow Celtic	1994	Dundee United
1968	Dunfermline Athletic	1995	Glasgow Celtic
1969	Glasgow Celtic	1996	Glasgow Rangers
1970	Aberdeen	1997	Kilmarnock
1971	Glasgow Celtic	1998	Heart Of Midlothian
1972	Glasgow Celtic	1999	Glasgow Rangers
1973	Glasgow Rangers	2000	Glasgow Rangers
1974	Glasgow Celtic	2001	Glasgow Celtic
1975	Glasgow Celtic	2002	Glasgow Rangers
1976	Glasgow Rangers	2003	Glasgow Rangers
1977	Glasgow Celtic	2004	Glasgow Celtic
1978	Glasgow Rangers		
1979	Glasgow Rangers		

European Champion Clubs Cup

Annual tournament for Europe's top domestic clubs. Founded in season 1955/56 and dominated throughout its early history by the Spanish giants Real Madrid. All previous winners listed. Season 1955/56 is indicated by the year 1956 and similarly for all other seasons.

Year	Winner	Year	Winner
1956	Real Madrid (ESP)	1979	Nottingham Forest (ENG)
1957	Real Madrid (ESP)	1980	Nottingham Forest (ENG)
1958	Real Madrid (ESP)	1981	Liverpool (ENG)
1959	Real Madrid (ESP)	1982	Aston Villa (ENG)
1960	Real Madrid (ESP)	1983	SV Hamburg (FRG)
1961	Benfica Lisbon (POR)	1984	Liverpool (ENG)
1962	Benfica Lisbon (POR)	1985	Juventus Turin (ITA)
1963	AC Milan (ITA)	1986	Steau Bucharest (ROM)
1964	Inter Milan (ITA)	1987	FC Porto (POR)
1965	Inter Milan (ITA)	1988	PSV Eindhoven (HOL)
1966	Real Madrid (ESP)	1989	AC Milan (ITA)
1967	Glasgow Celtic (SCO)	1990	AC Milan (ITA)
1968	Manchester Utd (ENG)	1991	Red Star Belgrade (YUG)
1969	AC Milan (ITA)	1992	FC Barcelona (ESP)
1970	Feyenoord Rotterdam (HOL)	1993	Olimpique Marseille (FRA)
1971	Ajax Amsterdam (HOL)	1994	AC Milan (ITA)
1972	Ajax Amsterdam (HOL)	1995	Ajax Amsterdam (HOL)
1973	Ajax Amsterdam (HOL)	1996	Juventus Turin (ITA)
1974	Bayern Munich (FRG)	1997	Borussia Dortmund (GER)
1975	Bayern Munich (FRG)	1998	Real Madrid (ESP)
1976	Bayern Munich (FRG)	1999	Manchester Utd (ENG)
1977	Liverpool (ENG)		
1978	Liverpool (ENG)		

2000	Real Madrid (ESP)	2003	AC Milan (ITA)
2001	Bayern Munich (GER)	2004	FC Porto (POR)
2002	Real Madrid (ESP)		

UEFA Cup

Consolation tournament for European clubs which finished high in their respective leagues but missed out on Champions Cup qualification. The inaugural tournament began in 1955 and finished in 1958, taking 3 years to complete, and the second commenced in 1958 and finished in 1960. Known as the Inter Cities Fairs Cup prior to 1971. All previous winners listed. Season 1960/61 is indicated by the year 1961 and similarly for all other seasons thereafter.

1958	FC Barcelona (ESP)	1973	Liverpool (ENG)
1960	FC Barcelona (ESP)	1974	Feyenoord Rotterdam (HOL)
1961	AS Roma (ITA)	1975	Borussia Moenchengladbach (FRG)
1962	Valencia CF (ESP)	1976	Liverpool (ENG)
1963	Valencia CF (ESP)	1977	Juventus Turin (ITA)
1964	Real Zaragoza (ESP)	1978	PSV Eindhoven (HOL)
1965	Ferencvaros (HUN)	1979	Borussia Moenchengladbach (FRG)
1966	FC Barcelona (ESP)	1980	Eintracht Frankfurt (FRG)
1967	Dynamo Zagreb (YUG)	1981	Ipswich Town (ENG)
1968	Leeds Utd (ENG)		
1969	Newcastle Utd (ENG)		
1970	Arsenal (ENG)		
1971	Leeds Utd (ENG)		
1972	Tottenham Hotspur (ENG)		

1982	IFK Gothenburg (SWE)	1994	Inter Milan (ITA)
1983	RSC Anderlecht (BEL)	1995	FC Parma (ITA)
1984	Tottenham Hotspur (ENG)	1996	Bayern Munich (GER)
1985	Real Madrid (ESP)	1997	Schalke 04 (GER)
1986	Real Madrid (ESP)	1998	Inter Milan (ITA)
1987	IFK Gothenburg (SWE)	1999	FC Parma (ITA)
1988	Bayer Leverkusen (FRG)	2000	Galatasaray (TUR)
1989	AC Napoli (ITA)	2001	Liverpool (ENG)
1990	Juventus Turin (ITA)	2002	Feyenoord Rotterdam (HOL)
1991	Inter Milan (ITA)	2003	FC Porto (POR)
1992	Ajax Amsterdam (HOL)	2004	Valencia (ESP)
1993	Juventus Turin (ITA)		

FIFA World Cup

The Holy Grail of world football was founded by FIFA in 1930 and is held every 4 years. It was cancelled in 1942 and 1946 due to World War II. All previous finals and venues are listed.

1930	Uruguay 4 Argentina 2 (*Montivideo, Uruguay*)
1934	Italy 2 Czechoslovakia 1 (aet) (*Rome, Italy*)
1938	Italy 4 Hungary 2 (*Paris, France*)
1950	Uruguay 2 Brazil 1 (*Rio de Janeiro, Brazil*)
1954	West Germany 3 Hungary 2 (*Berne, Switzerland*)
1958	Brazil 5 Sweden 2 (*Stockholm, Sweden*)
1962	Brazil 3 Czechoslovakia 1 (*Santiago, Chile*)
1966	England 4 West Germany 2 (aet) (*London, England*)
1970	Brazil 4 Italy 1 (*Mexico City, Mexico*)

1974	Germany 2 Holland 1 (*Munich, West Germany*)
1978	Argentina 3 Holland 1 (aet) (*Buenos Aries, Argentina*)
1982	Italy 3 West Germany 1 (*Madrid, Spain*)
1986	Argentina 3 West Germany 2 (*Mexico City, Mexico*)
1990	West Germany 1 Argentina 0 (*Rome, Italy*)
1994*	Brazil 0 Italy 0 (aet) (*Pasadena, USA*)
1998	France 3 Brazil 0 (*Paris, France*)
2002	Brazil 2 Germany 0 (*Yokohama, Japan*)

Note: The 1950 finals tournament was played on a league basis but was actually decided on the outcome of the final pool match between Uruguay and Brazil.

** Brazil won trophy following penalty kicks*

European International Championship

International tournament for all countries affiliated to UEFA and second only to the FIFA World Cup in terms of prestige. First final was held in 1960 and has been held every 4 years thereafter. All previous finals and venues are listed.

1960	Soviet Union 2 Yugoslavia 1 (aet) (*Paris, France*)
1964	Spain 2 Soviet Union 1 (*Madrid, Spain*)
1968	Italy 1 Yugoslavia 1 (aet) (*Rome, Italy*)
	Italy 2 Yugoslavia 0 (replay) (*Rome, Italy*)
1972	West Germany 3 Soviet Union 0 (*Brussels, Belgium*)
1976*	Czechoslovakia 2 West Germany 2 (aet) (*Belgrade, Yugoslavia*)
1980	West Germany 2 Belgium 1 (*Rome, Italy*)
1984	France 2 Spain 0 (*Paris, France*)

1988	Holland 2 Soviet Union 0 (*Munich, West Germany*)
1992	Denmark 2 Germany 0 (*Gothenburg, Sweden*)
1996	Germany 2 Czech Republic 1 (golden goal) (*London, England*)
2000	France 2 Italy 1 (golden goal) (*Rotterdam, Holland*)
2004	Greece 1 Portugal 0 (*Lisbon, Portugal*)

** Czechoslovakia won trophy following penalty kicks*

ATHLETICS

The Olympic Games

Founded by the French aristocrat Baron Pierre de Coubertin in 1896 and held, like their ancient equivalent, every 4 years. Venues and winners of main events from 1948.

1948	London, England	1980	Moscow, USSR
1952	Helsinki, Finland	1984	Los Angeles, USA
1956	Melbourne, Australia	1988	Seoul, South Korea
1960	Rome, Italy	1992	Barcelona, Spain
1964	Tokyo, Japan	1996	Atlanta, USA
1968	Mexico City, Mexico	2000	Sydney, Australia
1972	Munich, West Germany	2004	Athens, Greece
1976	Montreal, Canada	2008	Beijing, China

Men's 100 Metres		Sec
1948	H Dillard (USA)	10.3
1952	L Remigino (USA)	10.4
1956	R Morrow (USA)	10.5

Men's 100 Metres *cont.*		**Sec**
1960	A Hary (GER)	10.2
1964	B Hayes (USA)	10.0
1968	J Hines (USA)	9.95
1972	V Borsov (URS)	10.14
1976	H Crawford (TRI)	10.06
1980	A Wells (GBR)	10.25
1984	C Lewis (USA)	9.99
1988	C Lewis (USA)	9.92
1992	L Christie (GBR)	9.96
1996	D Bailey (CAN)	9.84
2000	M Greene (USA)	9.87
2004	J Gatlin (USA)	9.85

Men's 1500 Metres		**Min**
1948	H Eriksson (SWE)	3:49.8
1952	J Barthel (LUX)	3:45.2
1956	R Delany (IRL)	3:41.5
1960	H Elliott (AUS)	3:35.6
1964	P Snell (NZL)	3:38.1
1968	K Keino (KEN)	3:34.9
1972	P Vasala (FIN)	3:36.33
1976	J Walker (NZL)	3:39.17
1980	S Coe (GBR)	3:38.40
1984	S Coe (GBR)	3:32.53
1988	P Rono (KEN)	3:35.96
1992	F Cacho (ESP)	3:40.12
1996	N Morceli (ALG)	3:35.78
2000	N Ngeny (KEN)	3:33.07
2004	H El Guerrouj (MAR)	3:34.18

The Marathon 42.295 km		Hours
1948	D Cabrera (ARG)	2:34:51
1952	E Zatopek (TCH)	2:23:03
1956	A Mimoun (FRA)	2:25:00
1960	A Bikila (ETH)	2:15:16
1964	A Bikila (ETH)	2:12:11
1968	M Wolde (ETH)	2:20:26
1972	F Shorter (USA)	2:12:19
1976	W Cierpinski (GDR)	2:09:55
1980	W Cierpinski (GDR)	2:11:03
1984	C S Lopes (POR)	2:09:21
1988	G Bordin (ITA)	2:10:32
1992	H Young-Cho (KOR)	2:13:23
1996	J Thugwane (SAF)	2:12:36
2000	G Abera (ETH)	2:10:11
2004	S Baldini (ITA)	2:10:55

Women's 100 Metres		Sec
1948	F Blankers-Koen (HOL)	11.9
1952	M Jackson (AUS)	11.5
1956	B Cuthbert (AUS)	11.5
1960	W Rudolph (USA)	11.0
1964	W Tyus (USA)	11.4
1968	W Tyus (USA)	11.08
1972	R Stecher (GDR)	11.07
1976	A Richter (FRG)	11.08
1980	L Kondratyeva (URS)	11.06
1984	E Ashford (USA)	10.97
1988	F Griffith-Joyner (USA)	10.54
1992	G Devers (USA)	10.82
1996	G Devers (USA)	10.94
2000	M Jones (USA)	10.75
2004	Y Nesterenko (BLR)	10.93

Women's 1500 Metres (First held 1972)		Min
1972	L Bragina (URS)	4:01.38
1976	T Kazankina (URS)	4:05.48
1980	T Kazankina (URS)	3:56.56
1984	G Dorio (ITA)	4:03.25
1988	P Ivan (ROM)	3:53.96
1992	H Boulmerka (ALG)	3:55.30
1996	S Masterkova (RUS)	4:00.83
2000	N Merah-Benida (ALG)	4:05.10
2004	K Holmes (GBR)	3:57.90

Women's Marathon 42.295 km (First held 1984)		Hours
1984	J Benoit (USA)	2:24:52
1988	R Mota (POR)	2:25:40
1992	V Yegorova (CIS)	2:32:41
1996	F Roba (ETH)	2:26:05
2000	N Takahashi (JPN)	2:23:14
2004	M Noguchi (JPN)	2:26:20

BASEBALL

The World Series

End-of-season championship series, first held in 1903, between the respective winners of the American and National leagues to determine the official champions of Major League Baseball. Previous winners from 1949.

1949	New York Yankees	1953	New York Yankees
1950	New York Yankees	1954	New York Giants
1951	New York Yankees	1955	Brooklyn Dodgers
1952	New York Yankees	1956	New York Yankees

1957	Milwaukee Braves	1981	Los Angeles Dodgers
1958	New York Yankees	1982	St Louis Cardinals
1959	Los Angeles Dodgers	1983	Baltimore Orioles
1960	Pittsburgh Pirates	1984	Detroit Tigers
1961	New York Yankees	1985	Kansas City Royals
1962	New York Yankees	1986	New York Mets
1963	Los Angeles Dodgers	1987	Minnesota Twins
1964	St Louis Cardinals	1988	Los Angeles Dodgers
1965	Los Angeles Dodgers	1989	Oakland Athletics
1966	Baltimore Orioles	1990	Cincinnati Reds
1967	St Louis Cardinals	1991	Minnesota Twins
1968	Detroit Tigers	1992	Toronto Blue Jays
1969	New York Mets	1993	Toronto Blue Jays
1970	Baltimore Orioles	1994	Not Held
1971	Pittsburgh Pirates	1995	Atlanta Braves
1972	Oakland Athletics	1996	New York Yankees
1973	Oakland Athletics	1997	Florida Marlins
1974	Oakland Athletics	1998	New York Yankees
1975	Cincinnati Reds	1999	New York Yankees
1976	Cincinnati Reds	2000	New York Yankees
1977	New York Yankees	2001	Arizona Diamondbacks
1978	New York Yankees	2002	Anaheim Angels
1979	Pittsburgh Pirates	2003	Florida Marlins
1980	Philadelphia Phillies	2004	Boston Red Sox

BASKETBALL

American NBA Championship

The most prestigious event in professional basketball. Founded in season 1946/47 and first won by the Philadelphia Warriors. Previous winners from 1949 (Season 1948/49).

1949	Minneapolis Lakers	1977	Portland Trail Blazers
1950	Minneapolis Lakers	1978	Washington Bullets
1951	Rochester Royals	1979	Seattle Supersonics
1952	Minneapolis Lakers	1980	Los Angeles Lakers
1953	Minneapolis Lakers	1981	Boston Celtics
1954	Minneapolis Lakers	1982	Los Angeles Lakers
1955	Syracuse Nationals	1983	Philadelphia 76ers
1956	Philadelphia Warriors	1984	Boston Celtics
1957	Boston Celtics	1985	Los Angeles Lakers
1958	St Louis Hawks	1986	Boston Celtics
1959	Boston Celtics	1987	Los Angeles Lakers
1960	Boston Celtics	1988	Los Angeles Lakers
1961	Boston Celtics	1989	Detroit Pistons
1962	Boston Celtics	1990	Detroit Pistons
1963	Boston Celtics	1991	Chicago Bulls
1964	Boston Celtics	1992	Chicago Bulls
1965	Boston Celtics	1993	Chicago Bulls
1966	Boston Celtics	1994	Houston Rockets
1967	Philadelphia 76ers	1995	Houston Rockets
1968	Boston Celtics	1996	Chicago Bulls
1969	Boston Celtics	1997	Chicago Bulls
1970	New York Knicks	1998	Chicago Bulls
1971	Milwaukee Bucks	1999	San Antonio Spurs
1972	Los Angeles Lakers	2000	Los Angeles Lakers
1973	New York Knicks	2001	Los Angeles Lakers
1974	Boston Celtics	2002	Los Angeles Lakers
1975	Golden State Warriors	2003	San Antonio Spurs
1976	Boston Celtics	2004	Detroit Pistons

CRICKET

The County Championship

The first official championship was organized by the major counties in 1890. Before that 'unofficial' champions were declared by leading periodicals of the era. Previous winners from 1949.

1949	Middlesex/Yorkshire	1973	Hampshire
1950	Lancashire/Surrey	1974	Worcestershire
1951	Warwickshire	1975	Leicestershire
1952	Surrey	1976	Middlesex
1953	Surrey	1977	Kent/Middlesex
1954	Surrey	1978	Kent
1955	Surrey	1979	Essex
1956	Surrey	1980	Middlesex
1957	Surrey	1981	Nottinghamshire
1958	Surrey	1982	Middlesex
1959	Yorkshire	1983	Essex
1960	Yorkshire	1984	Essex
1961	Hampshire	1985	Middlesex
1962	Yorkshire	1986	Essex
1963	Yorkshire	1987	Nottinghamshire
1964	Worcestershire	1988	Worcestershire
1965	Worcestershire	1989	Worcestershire
1966	Yorkshire	1990	Middlesex
1967	Yorkshire	1991	Essex
1968	Yorkshire	1992	Essex
1969	Glamorgan	1993	Middlesex
1970	Kent	1994	Warwickshire
1971	Surrey	1995	Warwickshire
1972	Warwickshire	1996	Leicestershire

1997 Glamorgan	2001 Yorkshire
1998 Leicestershire	2002 Surrey
1999 Surrey	2003 Sussex
2000 Surrey	2004 Warwickshire

The Benson & Hedges Cup

First held in 1972 between the 17 first-class counties and combines from the minor counties. All previous winners listed.

1972 Leicestershire	1988 Hampshire
1973 Kent	1989 Nottinghamshire
1974 Surrey	1990 Lancashire
1975 Leicestershire	1991 Worcestershire
1976 Kent	1992 Hampshire
1977 Gloucestershire	1993 Derbyshire
1978 Kent	1994 Warwickshire
1979 Essex	1995 Lancashire
1980 Northamptonshire	1996 Lancashire
1981 Somerset	1997 Surrey
1982 Somerset	1998 Essex
1983 Middlesex	1999 Gloucestershire
1984 Lancashire	2000 Gloucestershire
1985 Leicestershire	2001 Surrey
1986 Middlesex	2002 Warwickshire
1987 Yorkshire	

Cheltenham & Gloucester Trophy

Founded in 1963 as the Gillette Cup and known as the NatWest Trophy 1981–2000. All previous winners listed.

1963	Sussex	1984	Middlesex
1964	Sussex	1985	Essex
1965	Yorkshire	1986	Sussex
1966	Warwickshire	1987	Nottinghamshire
1967	Kent	1988	Middlesex
1968	Warwickshire	1989	Warwickshire
1969	Yorkshire	1990	Lancashire
1970	Lancashire	1991	Hampshire
1971	Lancashire	1992	Northamptonshire
1972	Lancashire	1993	Warwickshire
1973	Gloucestershire	1994	Worcestershire
1974	Kent	1995	Warwickshire
1975	Lancashire	1996	Lancashire
1976	Northamptonshire	1997	Essex
1977	Middlesex	1998	Lancashire
1978	Sussex	1999	Gloucestershire
1979	Somerset	2000	Gloucestershire
1980	Middlesex	2001	Somerset
1981	Derbyshire	2002	Yorkshire
1982	Surrey	2003	Gloucestershire
1983	Somerset	2004	Gloucestershire

The World Cup

Founded in 1975 and now scheduled to be held every 4 years. All previous finals and venues are listed.

1975	West Indies beat Australia by 17 Runs (*England*)
1979	West Indies beat England by 92 Runs (*England*)
1983	India beat West Indies by 43 Runs (*England*)
1987	Australia beat England by 7 Runs (*India/Pakistan*)
1992	Pakistan beat England by 22 Runs (*Australia/New Zealand*)
1996	Sri Lanka beat Australia by 7 Wickets (*Pakistan/India/Sri Lanka*)
1999	Australia beat Pakistan by 8 Wickets (*England*)
2003	Australia beat India by 125 Runs (*South Africa/Zimbabwe*)

CYCLING

Tour de France

More people attend the Tour de France than any other sporting event in the world. Founded in 1903 by the French newspaper *L'Equipe* and first won by a Frenchman named Maurice Garin. Previous winners from 1949.

1949	F Coppi (ITA)	1959	F Bahamontes (ESP)
1950	F Kubler (SUI)	1960	G Nencini (ITA)
1951	H Koblet (SUI)	1961	J Anquetil (FRA)
1952	F Coppi (ITA)	1962	J Anquetil (FRA)
1953	L Bobet (FRA)	1963	J Anquetil (FRA)
1954	L Bobet (FRA)	1964	J Anquetil (FRA)
1955	L Bobet (FRA)	1965	F Gimondi (ITA)
1956	R Walkowiak (FRA)	1966	L Aimar (FRA)
1957	J Anquetil (FRA)	1967	R Pingeon (FRA)
1958	C Gaul (LUX)	1968	J Janssen (HOL)

1969	E Merckx (BEL)	1987	S Roche (IRL)
1970	E Merckx (BEL)	1988	P Delgado (ESP)
1971	E Merckx (BEL)	1989	G LeMond (USA)
1972	E Merckx (BEL)	1990	G LeMond (USA)
1973	L Ocana (ESP)	1991	M Indurain (ESP)
1974	E Merckx (BEL)	1992	M Indurain (ESP)
1975	B Thevenet (FRA)	1993	M Indurain (ESP)
1976	L Van Impe (BEL)	1994	M Indurain (ESP)
1977	B Thevenet (FRA)	1995	M Indurain (ESP)
1978	B Hinault (FRA)	1996	B Riis (DEN)
1979	B Hinault (FRA)	1997	J Ulrich (GER)
1980	J Zoetemelk (HOL)	1998	M Pantani (ITA)
1981	B Hinault (FRA)	1999	L Armstrong (USA)
1982	B Hinault (FRA)	2000	L Armstrong (USA)
1983	L Fignon (FRA)	2001	L Armstrong (USA)
1984	L Fignon (FRA)	2002	L Armstrong (USA)
1985	B Hinault (FRA)	2003	L Armstrong (USA)
1986	G LeMond (USA)	2004	L Armstrong (USA)

GOLF

The Open Championship

The oldest and most prestigious championship in golf. Founded at Prestwick in 1860 and first won by Willie Park snr. Previous winners from 1949.

1949 B Locke (SA)
1950 B Locke (SA)
1951 M Faulkner (GBR)
1952 B Locke (SA)
1953 B Hogan (USA)
1954 P Thomson (AUS)
1955 P Thomson (AUS)
1956 P Thomson (AUS)
1957 B Locke (SA)
1958 P Thomson (AUS)
1959 G Player (SA)
1960 K Nagle (AUS)
1961 A Palmer (USA)
1962 A Palmer (USA)
1963 B Charles (NZL)
1964 T Lema (USA)
1965 P Thomson (AUS)
1966 J Nicklaus (USA)
1967 R de Vicenzo (ARG)
1968 G Player (SA)
1969 T Jacklin (GBR)
1970 J Nicklaus (USA)
1971 L Trevino (USA)
1972 L Trevino (USA)
1973 T Weiskopf (USA)
1974 G Player (SA)
1975 T Watson (GBR)
1976 J Miller (USA)
1977 T Watson (USA)
1978 J Nicklaus (USA)
1979 S Ballesteros (ESP)
1980 T Watson (USA)
1981 B Rogers (USA)
1982 T Watson (USA)
1983 T Watson (USA)
1984 S Ballesteros (ESP)
1985 S Lyle (GBR)
1986 G Norman (AUS)
1987 N Faldo (GBR)
1988 S Ballesteros (ESP)
1989 M Calcavecchia (USA)
1990 N Faldo (GBR)
1991 I Baker-Finch (AUS)
1992 N Faldo (GBR)
1993 G Norman (AUS)
1994 N Price (ZIM)
1995 J Daly (USA)
1996 T Lehman (USA)
1997 J Leonard (USA)
1998 M O'Meara (USA)
1999 P Lawrie (GBR)
2000 T Woods (USA)
2001 D Duval (USA)
2002 E Els (SA)
2003 Ben Curtis (USA)
2004 Todd Hamilton (USA)

US Masters Tournament, Augusta

The first major championship of the year and the only one to be played at a permanent venue. Founded in 1934 by the legendary Bobby Jones, who also designed the famous Augusta course. Previous winners from 1949.

Year	Winner	Year	Winner
1949	S Snead (USA)	1975	J Nicklaus (USA)
1950	J Demaret (USA)	1976	R Floyd (USA)
1951	B Hogan (USA)	1977	T Watson (USA)
1952	S Snead (USA)	1978	G Player (SA)
1953	B Hogan (USA)	1979	F Zoeller (USA)
1954	S Snead (USA)	1980	S Ballesteros (ESP)
1955	C Middlecoff (USA)	1981	T Watson (USA)
1956	J Burke (USA)	1982	C Stadler (USA)
1957	D Ford (USA)	1983	S Ballesteros (ESP)
1958	A Palmer (USA)	1984	B Crenshaw (USA)
1959	A Wall jnr (USA)	1985	B Langer (FRG)
1960	A Palmer (USA)	1986	J Nicklaus (USA)
1961	G Player (SA)	1987	L Mize (USA)
1962	A Palmer (USA)	1988	S Lyle (GBR)
1963	J Nicklaus (USA)	1989	N Faldo (GBR)
1964	A Palmer (USA)	1990	N Faldo (GBR)
1965	J Nicklaus (USA)	1991	I Woosnam (GBR)
1966	J Nicklaus (USA)	1992	F Couples (USA)
1967	G Brewer (USA)	1993	B Langer (GER)
1968	B Goalby (USA)	1994	J-M Olazabal (ESP)
1969	G Archer (USA)	1995	B Crenshaw (USA)
1970	B Casper (USA)	1996	N Faldo (GBR)
1971	C Coody (USA)	1997	T Woods (USA)
1972	J Nicklaus (USA)	1998	M O'Meara (USA)
1973	T Aaron (USA)	1999	J-M Olazabal (ESP)
1974	G Player (SA)	2000	V Singh (FIJ)

2001	T Woods (USA)	2004	P Mickelson (USA)
2002	T Woods (USA)	2005	T Woods (USA)
2003	M Weir (CAN)		

US Open Championship

Founded in 1885 at Newport, Rhode Island by the United States Golf Association and first won by an American named Horace Rawlins. Previous winners from 1949.

1949	C Middlecoff (USA)	1971	L Trevino (USA)
1950	B Hogan (USA)	1972	J Nicklaus (USA)
1951	B Hogan (USA)	1973	J Miller (USA)
1952	J Boros (USA)	1974	H Irwin (USA)
1953	B Hogan (USA)	1975	L Graham (USA)
1954	E Furgol (USA)	1976	J Pate (USA)
1955	J Fleck (USA)	1977	H Green (USA)
1956	C Middlecoff (USA)	1978	A North (USA)
1957	D Mayer (USA)	1979	H Irwin (USA)
1958	T Bolt (USA)	1980	J Nicklaus (USA)
1959	B Casper (USA)	1981	D Graham (AUS)
1960	A Palmer (USA)	1982	T Watson (USA)
1961	G Littler (USA)	1983	L Nelson (USA)
1962	J Nicklaus (USA)	1984	F Zoeller (USA)
1963	J Boros (USA)	1985	A North (USA)
1964	K Venturi (USA)	1986	R Floyd (USA)
1965	G Player (SAF)	1987	S Simpson (USA)
1966	B Casper (USA)	1988	C Strange (USA)
1967	J Nicklaus (USA)	1989	C Strange (USA)
1968	L Trevino (USA)	1990	H Irwin (USA)
1969	O Moody (USA)	1991	P Stewart (USA)
1970	T Jacklin (GBR)	1992	T Kite (USA)

1993	L Janzen (USA)	1999	P Stewart (USA)
1994	E Els (SA)	2000	T Woods (USA)
1995	C Pavin (USA)	2001	R Goosen (SA)
1996	S Jones (USA)	2002	T Woods (USA)
1997	E Els (SA)	2003	J Furyk (USA)
1998	L Janzen (USA)	2004	R Goosen (SA)

USPGA Championship

Founded by the New York department store magnate Rodman Wanamaker in 1916 and first won by an American named James M Barnes. It was originally a match-play event until switching to stroke play in 1958. Previous winners from 1949.

1949	S Snead (USA)	1967	D January (USA)
1950	C Harper (USA)	1968	J Boros (USA)
1951	S Snead (USA)	1969	R Floyd (USA)
1952	J Turnesa (USA)	1970	D Stockton (USA)
1953	W Burkemo (USA)	1971	J Nicklaus (USA)
1954	C Harbert (USA)	1972	G Player (SA)
1955	D Ford (USA)	1973	J Nicklaus (USA)
1956	J Burke (USA)	1974	L Trevino (USA)
1957	L Herbert (USA)	1975	J Nicklaus (USA)
1958	D Finsterwald (USA)	1976	D Stockton (USA)
1959	B Rosburg (USA)	1977	L Wadkins (USA)
1960	J Herbert (USA)	1978	J Mahaffey (USA)
1961	J Barber (USA)	1979	D Graham (AUS)
1962	G Player (SA)	1980	J Nicklaus (USA)
1963	J Nicklaus (USA)	1981	L Nelson (USA)
1964	B Nichols (USA)	1982	R Floyd (USA)
1965	D Marr (USA)	1983	H Sutton (USA)
1966	A Geiberger (USA)	1984	L Trevino (USA)

1985	H Green (USA)	1995	S Elkington (AUS)
1986	B Tway (USA)	1996	M Brooks (USA)
1987	L Nelson (USA)	1997	D Love III (USA)
1988	J Sluman (USA)	1998	V Singh (FIJ)
1989	P Stewart (USA)	1999	T Woods (USA)
1990	W Grady (AUS)	2000	T Woods (USA)
1991	J Daly (USA)	2001	D Toms (USA)
1992	N Price (ZIM)	2002	R Beem (USA)
1993	P Azinger (USA)	2003	S Micheel (USA)
1994	N Price (ZIM)	2004	V Singh (FIJ)

The Ryder Cup

American millionaire Samuel Ryder, who made his fortune selling penny packets of flower seeds, founded the competition in 1927. It is a biennial event and staged alternately in America and Europe. United States v. Great Britain 1927–71, United States v. Great Britain & Ireland 1973–77 and United States v. Europe from 1979. It was not held during World War II and the 2001 competition was held over until 2002 following the September 11 tragedy in New York. Previous results in full.

Year	Winners (Captain)	Score	Losers (Captain)	Venue
1927	USA (W Hagen)	9½-2½	GBR (T Ray)	USA
1929	GBR (G Duncan)	07-05	USA (W Hagen)	UK
1931	USA (W Hagen)	09-03	GBR (C Whitcombe)	USA
1933	GBR (J H Taylor*)	6½-5½	USA (W Hagen)	UK
1935	USA (W Hagen)	09-03	GBR (C Whitcombe)	USA
1937	USA (W Hagen*)	08-04	GBR (C Whitcombe)	UK
1947	USA (B Hogan)	11-01	GBR (H Cotton)	USA

Year	Winners (Captain)	Score	Losers (Captain)	Venue
1949	USA (B Hogan*)	07-05	GBR (C Whitcombe*)	UK
1951	USA (S Snead)	$9\frac{1}{2}$-$2\frac{1}{2}$	GBR (A Lacey*)	USA
1953	USA (L Mangrum)	$6\frac{1}{2}$-$5\frac{1}{2}$	GBR (A Lacey*)	UK
1955	USA (C Harbert)	08-04	GBR (D Rees)	USA
1957	GBR (D Rees)	$7\frac{1}{2}$-$4\frac{1}{2}$	USA (J Burke)	UK
1959	USA (S Snead)	$8\frac{1}{2}$-$3\frac{1}{2}$	GBR (D Rees)	USA
1961	USA (J Barber)	$14\frac{1}{2}$-$9\frac{1}{2}$	GBR (D Rees)	UK
1963	USA (A Palmer)	23-09	GBR (J Fallon*)	USA
1965	USA (B Nelson*)	$19\frac{1}{2}$-$12\frac{1}{2}$	GBR (H Weetman*)	UK
1967	USA (B Hogan*)	23-$8\frac{1}{2}$	GBR (D Rees*)	USA
1969†	USA (S Snead*)	16-16	GBR (E Brown*)	UK
1971	USA (J Herbert*)	$18\frac{1}{2}$-$13\frac{1}{2}$	GBR (E Brown*)	USA
1973	USA (J Burke*)	19-13	GBI (B Hunt*)	UK
1975	USA (A Palmer*)	21-11	GBI (B Hunt*)	USA
1977	USA (D Finsterwald)	$12\frac{1}{2}$-$7\frac{1}{2}$	GBI (B Huggett*)	UK
1979	USA (B Casper*)	17-11	EUR (B Hunt*)	USA
1981	USA (D Marr*)	$18\frac{1}{2}$-$9\frac{1}{2}$	EUR (J Jacobs*)	UK
1983	USA (J Nicklaus*)	$14\frac{1}{2}$-$13\frac{1}{2}$	EUR (T Jacklin*)	USA
1985	EUR (T Jacklin*)	$16\frac{1}{2}$-$11\frac{1}{2}$	USA (L Trevino*)	UK
1987	EUR (T Jacklin*)	15-13	USA (J Nicklaus*)	USA
1989†	EUR (T Jacklin*)	14-14	USA (R Floyd*)	UK
1991	USA (D Stockton*)	$14\frac{1}{2}$-$13\frac{1}{2}$	EUR (B Gallacher*)	USA
1993	USA (T Watson*)	15-13	EUR (B Gallacher*)	UK
1995	EUR (B Gallacher*)	$14\frac{1}{2}$-$13\frac{1}{2}$	USA (L Wadkins*)	USA
1997	EUR (S Ballesteros*)	$14\frac{1}{2}$-$13\frac{1}{2}$	USA (T Kite*)	Spain
1999	USA (B Crenshaw*)	$14\frac{1}{2}$-$13\frac{1}{2}$	EUR (M James*)	USA
2002	EUR (S Torrance*)	15-13	USA (C Strange*)	UK
2004	EUR (B Langer*)	18.5-9.5	USA (H Sutton*)	USA

† Retained trophy following tied match

** Denotes non-playing Captain*

HORSE RACING

The Derby Stakes, Epsom, 1 mile 4 furlongs

The Blue Riband of the Turf. Founded in 1780 by the 12th Earl of Derby who evidently tossed a coin with his friend Sir Charles Bunbury to decide after whom the race would be named. For 3-year-old colts and fillies only. Previous winners from 1949.

1949	Nimbus	1972	Roberto
1950	Galcador	1973	Morston
1951	Arctic Prince	1974	Snow Knight
1952	Tulyar	1975	Grundy
1953	Pinza	1976	Empery
1954	Never Say Die	1977	The Minstrel
1955	Phil Drake	1978	Shirley Heights
1956	Lavandin	1979	Troy
1957	Crepello	1980	Henbit
1958	Hard Ridden	1981	Shergar
1959	Parthia	1982	Golden Fleece
1960	St Paddy	1983	Teenoso
1961	Psidium	1984	Secreto
1962	Larkspur	1985	Slip Anchor
1963	Relko	1986	Shahrastani
1964	Santa Claus	1987	Reference Point
1965	Sea Bird II	1988	Kahyasi
1966	Charlottown	1989	Nashwan
1967	Royal Palace	1990	Quest For Fame
1968	Sir Ivor	1991	Generous
1969	Blakeney	1992	Dr Devious
1970	Nijinsky	1993	Commander In Chief
1971	Mill Reef	1994	Erhaab

1995	Lammtarra	2000	Sinndar
1996	Shaamit	2001	Galileo
1997	Benny The Dip	2002	High Chaparral
1998	High-Rise	2003	Kris Kin
1999	Oath	2004	North Light

The Oaks Stakes, Epsom, 1 mile 4 furlongs

Founded in 1779 by the 12th Earl of Derby and named after his Epsom country house where he entertained his friends attending the nearby races. For 3-year-old fillies only. Previous winners from 1949.

1949	Musidora	1969	Sleeping Partner
1950	Asmena	1970	Lupe
1951	Neasham Belle	1971	Altesse Royale
1952	Frieze	1972	Ginevra
1953	Ambiguity	1973	Mysterious
1954	Sun Cap	1974	Polygamy
1955	Meld	1975	Juliette Marny
1956	Sicarelle	1976	Pawneese
1957	Carrozza	1977	Dunfermline
1958	Bella Paola	1978	Fair Salinia
1959	Petite Etoile	1979	Scintillate
1960	Never Too Late	1980	Bireme
1961	Sweet Solera	1981	Blue Wind
1962	Monade	1982	Time Charter
1963	Noblesse	1983	Sun Princess
1964	Homeward Bound	1984	Circus Plume
1965	Long Look	1985	Oh So Sharp
1966	Valoris	1986	Midway Lady
1967	Pia	1987	Unite
1968	La Lagune	1988	Diminuendo

1989* Snow Bride	1997 Reams Of Verse
1990 Salsabil	1998 Shantoush
1991 Jet Ski Lady	1999 Ramruma
1992 User Friendly	2000 Love Divine
1993 Intrepidity	2001 Imagine
1994 Balanchine	2002 Kazzia
1995 Moonshell	2003 Casual Look
1996 Lady Carla	2004 Ouija Board

** Alysya finished first but was later disqualified*

1,000 Guineas Stakes, Newmarket, 1 mile

Founded by the Jockey Club in 1814 and first won by a filly named Charlotte. For 3-year-old fillies only. Previous winners from 1949.

1949 Musidora	1967 Fleet
1950 Camaree	1968 Caergwrle
1951 Belle Of All	1969 Full Dress II
1952 Zabara	1970 Humble Duty
1953 Happy Laughter	1971 Altesse Royale
1954 Festoon	1972 Waterloo
1955 Meld	1973 Mysterious
1956 Honeylight	1974 Highclere
1957 Rose Royalè II	1975 Nocturnal Spree
1958 Bella Paola	1976 Flying Water
1959 Petite Etoile	1977 Mrs McArdy
1960 Never Too Late II	1978 Enstone Spark
1961 Sweet Solera	1979 One In A Million
1962 Abermaid	1980 Quick As Lightning
1963 Hula Dancer	1981 Fairy Footsteps
1964 Pourparier	1982 On The House
1965 Night Off	1983 Ma Biche
1966 Glad Rags	1984 Pebbles

1985	Oh So Sharp	1996	Bosra Sham
1986	Midway Lady	1997	Sleepytime
1987	Miesque	1998	Cape Verdi
1988	Ravinella	1999	Wince
1989	Musical Bliss	2000	Lahan
1990	Salsabil	2001	Ameerat
1991	Shadayid	2002	Kazzia
1992	Hatoof	2003	Russian Rhythm
1993	Sayyedati	2004	Attraction
1994	Las Meninas	2005	Virginia Water
1995	Harayir		

2,000 Guineas Stakes, Newmarket, 1 mile

Founded by the Jockey Club in 1809 and first won by a horse named Wizard. For 3-year-old colts and fillies only. Previous winners from 1949.

1949	Nimbus	1964	Baldric
1950	Palestine	1965	Niksar
1951	Ki Ming	1966	Kashmir
1952	Thunderhead	1967	Royal Palace
1953	Nearula	1968	Sir Ivor
1954	Darius	1969	Right Tack
1955	Our Babu	1970	Nijinsky
1956	Gilles de Retz	1971	Brigadier Gerard
1957	Crepello	1972	High Top
1958	Pall Mall	1973	Mon Fils
1959	Taboun	1974	Nonoalco
1960	Martial	1975	Bolkonski
1961	Rockavon	1976	Wollow
1962	Privy Councillor	1977	Nebbiolo
1963	Only For Life	1978	Roland Gardens

1979 Tap On Wood	1993 Zafonic
1980* Known Fact	1994 Mister Baileys
1981 To-Agori-Mou	1995 Pennekamp
1982 Zino	1996 Mark Of Esteem
1983 Lomond	1997 Entrepreneur
1984 El Gran Senor	1998 King Of Kings
1985 Shadeed	1999 Island Sands
1986 Dancing Brave	2000 King's Best
1987 Dont Forget Me	2001 Golan
1988 Doyoun	2002 Rock Of Gibraltar
1989 Nashwan	2003 Refuse to Bend
1990 Tirol	2004 Haafhd
1991 Mystiko	2005 Footsteps in the Sand
1992 Rodrigo De Triano	

** Nureyef finished first but was later disqualified*

St Leger Stakes, Doncaster, 1 mile 6 furlongs

The oldest Classic horse race in the world. First run in 1776 and named after its founder Colonel Anthony St Leger. For 3-year-old colts and fillies only. Previous winners from 1949.

1949 Ridge Wood	1959 Cantelo
1950 Scratch	1960 St Paddy
1951 Talma	1961 Aurelius
1952 Tulyar	1962 Heathersett
1953 Premonition	1963 Ragusa
1954 Never Say Die	1964 Indiana
1955 Meld	1965 Provoke
1956 Cambremer	1966 Sodium
1957 Ballymoss	1967 Ribocco
1958 Alcide	1968 Ribero

1969	Intermezzo	1987	Reference Point
1970	Nijinsky	1988	Minster Son
1971	Athens Wood	1989*	Michelozzo
1972	Boucher	1990	Snurge
1973	Peleid	1991	Toulon
1974	Bustino	1992	User Friendly
1975	Bruni	1993	Bob's Return
1976	Crow	1994	Moonax
1977	Dunfermline	1995	Classic Cliche
1978	Julio Mariner	1996	Shantou
1979	Son Of Love	1997	Silver Patriarch
1980	Light Cavalry	1998	Nedawi
1981	Cut Above	1999	Mutafaweq
1982	Touching Wood	2000	Millenary
1983	Sun Princess	2001	Milan
1984	Commanche Run	2002	Bollin Eric
1985	Oh So Sharp	2003	Brian Boru
1986	Moon Madness	2004	Rule of Law

**Race run at Ayr*

The Champion Hurdle Challenge Cup, Cheltenham, 2 miles

Run in March each year to determine Europe's official top hurdler. First run in 1927 and won by a horse named Blaris. Previous winners from 1949.

1949	Hatton's Grace	1956	Doorknocker
1950	Hatton's Grace	1957	Merry Deal
1951	Hatton's Grace	1958	Bandalore
1952	Sir Ken	1959	Fare Time
1953	Sir Ken	1960	Another Flash
1954	Sir Ken	1961	Eborneezer
1955	Clair Soleil	1962	Anzio

1963	Winning Fair	1985	See You Then
1964	Magic Court	1986	See You Then
1965	Kirriemuir	1987	See You Then
1966	Salmon Spray	1988	Celtic Shot
1967	Saucy Kit	1989	Beech Road
1968	Persian War	1990	Kribensis
1969	Persian War	1991	Morley Street
1970	Persian War	1992	Royal Gait
1971	Bula	1993	Granville Again
1972	Bula	1994	Flakey Dove
1973	Comedy Of Errors	1995	Alderbrook
1974	Lanzarote	1996	Collier Bay
1975	Comedy Of Errors	1997	Make A Stand
1976	Night Nurse	1998	Istabraq
1977	Night Nurse	1999	Istabraq
1978	Monksfield	2000	Istabraq
1979	Monksfield	2001	Race Not Run
1980	Sea Pigeon	2002	Hors La Loi
1981	Sea Pigeon	2003	Rooster Booster
1982	For Auction	2004	Hardy Eustace
1983	Gaye Brief	2005	Hardy Eustace
1984	Dawn Run		

Cheltenham Gold Cup Steeplechase, Cheltenham, 3 miles 2 furlongs

The Blue Riband event of National Hunt racing. First run in 1924 and won by a horse named Red Splash. Previous winners from 1949.

1949	Cottage Rake	1953	Knock Hard
1950	Cottage Rake	1954	Four Ten
1951	Silver Fame	1955	Gay Donald
1952	Mont Tremblant	1956	Limber Hill

1957	Linwell	1982	Silver Buck
1958	Kerstin	1983	Bregawn
1959	Roddy Owen	1984	Burrough Hill Lad
1960	Pas Seul	1985	Forgive N Forget
1961	Saffron Tartan	1986	Dawn Run
1962	Mandarin	1987	The Thinker
1963	Mill House	1988	Charter Party
1964	Arkle	1989	Desert Orchid
1965	Arkle	1990	Nortons Coin
1966	Arkle	1991	Garrison Savannah
1967	Woodland Venture	1992	Cool Ground
1968	Fort Leney	1993	Jodami
1969	What A Myth	1994	The Fellow
1970	L'Escargot	1995	Master Oats
1971	L'Escargot	1996	Imperial Call
1972	Glencaraig Lady	1997	Mr Mulligan
1973	The Dikler	1998	Cool Dawn
1974	Captain Christy	1999	See More Business
1975	Ten Up	2000	Looks Like Trouble
1976	Royal Frolic	2001	Race Not Run
1977	Davy Lad	2002	Best Mate
1978	Midnight Court	2003	Best Mate
1979	Alverton	2004	Best Mate
1980*	Master Smudge	2005	Kicking King
1981	Little Owl		

** Tied Cottage finished first but was later disqualified*

Grand National Steeplechase, Aintree, 4 miles 4 furlongs

The most famous horse race in the world. Founded by Liverpool hotelier William Lynn at Maghull in 1837 and first won by a horse named The Duke. Switched across the city to Aintree in 1839. Previous winners from 1949.

1949	Russian Hero	1978	Lucius
1950	Freebooter	1979	Rubstic
1951	Nickel Coin	1980	Ben Nevis
1952	Teal	1981	Aldaniti
1953	Early Mist	1982	Grittar
1954	Royal Tan	1983	Corbiere
1955	Quare Times	1984	Hallo Dandy
1956	ESB	1985	Last Suspect
1957	Sundew	1986	West Tip
1958	Mr What	1987	Maori Venture
1959	Oxo	1988	Rhyme N Reason
1960	Merryman II	1989	Little Polveir
1961	Nicolaus Silver	1990	Mr Frisk
1962	Kilmore	1991	Seagram
1963	Ayala	1992	Party Politics
1964	Team Spirit	1993	Race Declared Void
1965	Jay Trump	1994	Miinnehoma
1966	Anglo	1995	Royal Athlete
1967	Foinavon	1996	Rough Quest
1968	Red Alligator	1997	Lord Gyllene
1969	Highland Wedding	1998	Earth Summit
1970	Gay Trip	1999	Bobbyjo
1971	Specify	2000	Papillon
1972	Well To Do	2001	Red Marauder
1973	Red Rum	2002	Bindaree
1974	Red Rum	2003	Monty`s Pass
1975	L'Escargot	2004	Amberleigh House
1976	Rag Trade	2005	Hedgehunter
1977	Red Rum		

MOTOR RACING

F1 World Drivers' Championship

Grand Prix races have taken place since the beginning of the 20th century but it was not until 1950 that motor racing as we know it today evolved with the founding of the F1 World Drivers' Championship. All previous winners listed.

1950	G Farina (ITA)	Alfa Romeo
1951	J-M Fangio (ARG)	Alfa Romeo
1952	A Ascari (ITA)	Ferrari
1953	A Ascari (ITA)	Ferrari
1954	J-M Fangio (ARG)	Maserati
1955	J-M Fangio (ARG)	Mercedes-Benz
1956	J-M Fangio (ARG)	Lancia-Ferrari
1957	J-M Fangio (ARG)	Maserati
1958	M Hawthorn (GBR)	Ferrari
1959	J Brabham (AUS)	Cooper-Climax
1960	J Brabham (AUS)	Cooper-Climax
1961	P Hill (USA)	Ferrari
1962	G Hill (GBR)	BRM
1963	J Clark (GBR)	Lotus-Climax
1964	J Surtees (GBR)	Ferrari
1965	J Clark (GBR)	Lotus-Climax
1966	J Brabham (AUS)	Brabham-Repco
1967	D Hulme (NZL)	Brabham-Repco
1968	G Hill (GBR)	Lotus-Ford
1969	J Stewart (GBR)	Matra-Ford
1970	J Rindt (AUT)	Lotus-Ford
1971	J Stewart (GBR)	Tyrrell-Ford
1972	E Fittipaldi (BRA)	Lotus-Ford

1973	J Stewart (GBR)	Tyrrell-Ford
1974	E Fittipaldi (BRA)	McLaren-Ford
1975	N Lauda (AUT)	Ferrari
1976	J Hunt (GBR)	McLaren-Ford
1977	N Lauda (AUT)	Ferrari
1978	M Andretti (USA)	Lotus-Ford
1979	J Scheckter (SA)	Ferrari
1980	A Jones (AUS)	Williams-Ford
1981	N Piquet (BRA)	Brabham-Cosworth
1982	K Rosberg (FIN)	Williams-Cosworth
1983	N Piquet (BRA)	Brabham-BMW
1984	N Lauda (AUT)	McLaren-TAG-Porsche
1985	A Prost (FRA)	McLaren-TAG-Porsche
1986	A Prost (FRA)	McLaren-TAG-Porsche
1987	N Piquet (BRA)	Williams-Honda
1988	A Senna (BRA)	McLaren-Honda
1989	A Prost (FRA)	McLaren-Honda
1990	A Senna (BRA)	McLaren-Honda
1991	A Senna (BRA)	McLaren-Honda
1992	N Mansell (GBR)	Williams-Renault
1993	A Prost (FRA)	Williams-Renault
1994	M Schumacher (GER)	Benetton-Ford
1995	M Schumacher (GER)	Benetton-Renault
1996	D Hill (GBR)	Williams-Renault
1997	J Villeneuve (CAN)	Williams-Renault
1998	M Hakkinen (FIN)	McLaren-Mercedes
1999	M Hakkinen (FIN)	McLaren-Mercedes
2000	M Schumacher (GER)	Ferrari
2001	M Schumacher (GER)	Ferrari
2002	M Schumacher (GER)	Ferrari
2003	M Schumacher (GER)	Ferrari
2004	M Schumacher (GER)	Ferrari

RUGBY LEAGUE

The Challenge Cup

Rugby League's oldest club tournament was first won in season 1897/98 by Batley who defeated St Helens 10-03 at Headingley in Leeds. Previous winners from 1949 (Season 1948/49).

Year	Winner
1949	Bradford Northern
1950	Warrington
1951	Wigan
1952	Workington Town
1953	Huddersfield
1954	Warrington
1955	Barrow
1956	St Helens
1957	Leeds
1958	Wigan
1959	Wigan
1960	Wakefield Trinity
1961	St Helens
1962	Wakefield Trinity
1963	Wakefield Trinity
1964	Widnes
1965	Wigan
1966	St Helens
1967	Featherstone Rovers
1968	Leeds
1969	Castleford
1970	Castleford
1971	Leigh
1972	St Helens
1973	Featherstone Rovers
1974	Warrington
1975	Widnes
1976	St Helens
1977	Leeds
1978	Leeds
1979	Widnes
1980	Hull Kingston Rovers
1981	Widnes
1982	Hull
1983	Featherstone Rovers
1984	Widnes
1985	Wigan
1986	Castleford
1987	Halifax
1988	Wigan
1989	Wigan
1990	Wigan
1991	Wigan
1992	Wigan
1993	Wigan
1994	Wigan
1995	Wigan
1996	St Helens
1997	St Helens
1998	Sheffield Eagles

1999	Leeds Rhinos	2002	Wigan Warriors
2000	Bradford Bulls	2003	Bradford Bulls
2001	St Helens	2004	St Helens

The Super League

A new era in Rugby League began in 1996 when media magnate Rupert Murdoch sank millions into the game and established Sky's Super League. In 1998 the league adopted the Australian play-off format, culminating with the Grand Final, to determine the outright winners. All previous winners listed.

1996	St Helens	2001	Bradford Bulls
1997	Bradford Bulls	2002	St Helens
1998	Wigan Warriors	2003	Bradford Bulls
1999	St Helens	2004	Leeds Rhinos
2000	St Helens		

The World Cup

First held in 1954 following an idea put forward by French Rugby League president Paul Barrière. All previous winners listed.

1954	Great Britain	1975	Australia
1957	Australia	1977	Australia
1960	Great Britain	1988	Australia
1968	Australia	1992	Australia
1970	Australia	1995	Australia
1972	Great Britain	2000	Australia

RUGBY UNION

6 Nations Championship

Founded in 1883 as the Home International Championship. Became known as the 5 Nations Championship when France joined the competition in 1910 and as the 6 Nations Championship when Italy entered the fray in 2000. Previous winners from 1949.

1949	Ireland	1972	Wales
1950	Wales	1973	Quintuple Tie
1951	Ireland	1974	Ireland
1952	Wales	1975	Wales
1953	England	1976	Wales
1954	England/France/Wales	1977	France
1955	France/Wales	1978	Wales
1956	Wales	1979	Wales
1957	England	1980	England
1958	England	1981	France
1959	France	1982	Ireland
1960	France/England	1983	Ireland/France
1961	France	1984	Scotland
1962	France	1985	Ireland
1963	England	1986	France/Scotland
1964	Scotland/Wales	1987	France
1965	Wales	1988	France/Wales
1966	Wales	1989	France
1967	France	1990	Scotland
1968	France	1991	England
1969	Wales		
1970	Wales/France		
1971	Wales		

1992	England	1999	Scotland
1993	France	2000	England
1994	Wales	2001	England
1995	England	2002	France
1996	England	2003	England
1997	France	2004	France
1998	France	2005	Wales

The World Cup

The competition was founded in 1987 and was the brainchild of Australian legend Harry Tolhurst. It is held every 4 years. Results of all previous finals are listed.

1987	New Zealand 29 France 9 (*Auckland, New Zealand*)
1991	Australia 12 England 6 (*Twickenham, England*)
1995	South Africa 15 New Zealand 12 (*Johannesburg, South Africa*)
1999	Australia 35 France 12 (*Cardiff, Wales*)
2003	England 20 Australia 17 (aet) (*Sydney, Australia*)

Grand Slam Winners

England (11)	1913, 1914, 1921, 1923, 1924, 1928, 1957, 1980, 1991, 1995, 2003
France (7)	1968, 1977, 1981, 1987, 1997, 1998, 2002
Wales (7)	1911, 1950, 1952, 1971, 1976, 1978, 2005
Scotland (3)	1925, 1984, 1990
Ireland (1)	1948

Triple Crown Winners

England (22)	1883, 1884, 1892, 1913, 1914, 1921, 1923, 1924, 1928, 1934, 1937, 1954, 1957, 1960, 1980, 1991, 1995, 1996, 1997, 1998, 2002, 2003
Wales (18)	1893, 1900, 1902, 1905, 1908, 1909, 1911, 1950, 1952, 1965, 1969, 1971, 1976, 1977, 1978, 1979, 1988, 2005
Scotland (10)	1891, 1895, 1901, 1903, 1907, 1925, 1933, 1938, 1984, 1990
Ireland (7)	1894, 1899, 1948, 1949, 1982, 1985, 2004

SNOOKER

The World Professional Championship

First held in 1927 at Camkins Hall, Birmingham where the legendary Joe Davis beat Tom Dennis 20–11. The championship, as we know it today, first took shape in 1977 when the WPBSA decided to hold it permanently at The Crucible Theatre, Sheffield. Previous winners from 1977.

1977	J Spencer (ENG)
1978	R Reardon (WAL)
1979	T Griffiths (WAL)
1980	C Thorburn (CAN)
1981	S Davis (ENG)
1982	A Higgins (IRL)
1983	S Davis (ENG)
1984	S Davis (ENG)
1985	D Taylor (IRL)
1986	J Johnson (ENG)
1987	S Davis (ENG)
1988	S Davis (ENG)
1989	S Davis (ENG)
1990	S Hendry (SCO)
1991	J Parrott (ENG)
1992	S Hendry (SCO)

1993	S Hendry (SCO)	2000	M Williams (WAL)
1994	S Hendry (SCO)	2001	R O'Sullivan (ENG)
1995	S Hendry (SCO)	2002	P Ebdon (ENG)
1996	S Hendry (SCO)	2003	M Williams (WAL)
1997	K Doherty (IRL)	2004	R O'Sullivan (ENG)
1998	J Higgins (SCO)	2005	S Murphy (ENG)
1999	S Hendry (SCO)		

TENNIS

Wimbledon Open Championships

The oldest and most prestigious tennis championships in the world. Men's Singles first won by S W Gore in 1877 and Women's Singles by M E Watson in 1884. Previous winners from 1949.

Men's Singles

1949	T Schroeder (USA)
1950	B Patty (USA)
1951	R Savitt (USA)
1952	F Sedgman (AUS)
1953	V Seixas (USA)
1954	J Drobny (EGY)
1955	T Trabert (USA)
1956	L Hoad (AUS)
1957	L Hoad (AUS)
1958	A Cooper (AUS)
1959	A Olmedo (USA)
1960	N Fraser (AUS)

Women's Singles

1949	A L Brough (USA)
1950	A L Brough (USA)
1951	D Hart (USA)
1952	M Connolly (USA)
1953	M Connolly (USA)
1954	M Connolly (USA)
1955	A L Brough (USA)
1956	S Fry (USA)
1957	A Gibson (USA)
1958	A Gibson (USA)
1959	M Bueno (BRA)
1960	M Bueno (BRA)

Men's Singles *cont.*

Year	Winner
1961	R Laver (AUS)
1962	R Laver (AUS)
1963	C McKinley (USA)
1964	R Emerson (AUS)
1965	R Emerson (AUS)
1966	M Santana (ESP)
1967	J Newcombe (AUS)
1968	R Laver (AUS)
1969	R Laver (AUS)
1970	J Newcombe (AUS)
1971	J Newcombe (AUS)
1972	S Smith (USA)
1973	J Kodes (TCH)
1974	J Connors (USA)
1975	A Ashe (USA)
1976	B Borg (SWE)
1977	B Borg (SWE)
1978	B Borg (SWE)
1979	B Borg (SWE)
1980	B Borg (SWE)
1981	J P McEnroe (USA)
1982	J Connors (USA)
1983	J P McEnroe (USA)
1984	J P McEnroe (USA)
1985	B Becker (FRG)
1986	B Becker (FRG)
1987	P Cash (AUS)
1988	S Edberg (SWE)

Women's Singles *cont.*

Year	Winner
1961	A Mortimer (GBR)
1962	K Susman (USA)
1963	M Smith (AUS)
1964	M Bueno (BRA)
1965	M Smith (AUS)
1966	B J King (USA)
1967	B J King (USA)
1968	B J King (USA)
1969	A Jones (GBR)
1970	M Court (AUS)
1971	E Goolagong (AUS)
1972	B J King (USA)
1973	B J King (USA)
1974	C Evert (USA)
1975	B J King (USA)
1976	C Evert (USA)
1977	V Wade (GBR)
1978	M Navratilova (TCH)
1979	M Navratilova (TCH)
1980	E Cawley (AUS)
1981	C Evert-Lloyd (USA)
1982	M Navratilova (USA)
1983	M Navratilova (USA)
1984	M Navratilova (USA)
1985	M Navratilova (USA)
1986	M Navratilova (USA)
1987	M Navratilova (USA)
1988	S Graf (FRG)

Men's Singles *cont.*

1989	B Becker (FRG)
1990	S Edberg (SWE)
1991	M Stich (GER)
1992	A Agassi (USA)
1993	P Sampras (USA)
1994	P Sampras (USA)
1995	P Sampras (USA)
1996	R Krajicek (HOL)
1997	P Sampras (USA)
1998	P Sampras (USA)
1999	P Sampras (USA)
2000	P Sampras (USA)
2001	G Ivanisevic (CRO)
2002	L Hewitt (AUS)
2003	R Federer (SUI)
2004	R Federer (SUI)

Women's Singles *cont.*

1989	S Graf (FRG)
1990	M Navratilova (USA)
1991	S Graf (FRG)
1992	S Graf (GER)
1993	S Graf (GER)
1994	C Martinez (ESP)
1995	S Graf (GER)
1996	S Graf (GER)
1997	M Hingis (SUI)
1998	J Novotna (TCH)
1999	L Davenport (USA)
2000	V Williams (USA)
2001	V Williams (USA)
2002	S Williams (USA)
2003	S Williams (USA)
2004	M Sharapova (RUS)

Australian Open Championships

Held at Flinders Park, Melbourne in January each year, the Australian Open Championships herald the start of the new season. Men's Singles first won by R W Heath in 1905 and Women's Singles by M Molesworth in 1922. Previous winners from 1979.

Men's Singles

Year	Winner
1979	G Vilas (ARG)
1980	B Teacher (USA)
1981	J Kriek (SA)
1982	J Kriek (SA)
1983	M Wilander (SWE)
1984	M Wilander (SWE)
1985	S Edberg (SWE)
1986	Not Held
1987	S Edberg (SWE)
1988	M Wilander (SWE)
1989	I Lendl (TCH)
1990	I Lendl (TCH)
1991	B Becker (GER)
1992	J Courier (USA)
1993	J Courier (USA)
1994	P Sampras (USA)
1995	A Agassi (USA)
1996	B Becker (GER)
1997	P Sampras (USA)
1998	P Korda (TCH)
1999	Y Kafelnikov (RUS)
2000	A Agassi (USA)

Women's Singles

Year	Winner
1979	B Jordan (USA)
1980	H Mandlikova (TCH)
1981	M Navratilova (TCH)
1982	C Evert-Lloyd (USA)
1983	M Navratilova (USA)
1984	C Evert-Lloyd (USA)
1985	M Navratilova (USA)
1986	Not Held
1987	H Mandlikova (TCH)
1988	S Graf (FRG)
1989	S Graf (FRG)
1990	S Graf (FRG)
1991	M Seles (YUG)
1992	M Seles (YUG)
1993	M Seles (CRO)
1994	S Graf (GER)
1995	M Pierce (FRA)
1996	M Seles (USA)
1997	M Hingis (SUI)
1998	M Hingis (SUI)
1999	M Hingis (SUI)
2000	L Davenport (USA)

Men's Singles *cont.*	
2001	A Agassi (USA)
2002	T Johansson (SWE)
2003	A Agassi (USA)
2004	R Federer (SUI)
2005	M Safin (RUS)

Women's Singles *cont.*	
2001	J Capriati (USA)
2002	J Capriati (USA)
2003	S Williams (USA)
2004	J Henin-Hardenne (BEL)
2005	S Williams (USA)

French Open Championships

Entries from outside France were first accepted in 1925 when the Men's and Women's Singles were won by R Lacoste and S Lenglen respectively. Previous winners from 1979.

Men's Singles	
1979	B Borg (SWE)
1980	B Borg (SWE)
1981	B Borg (SWE)
1982	M Wilander (SWE)
1983	Y Noah (FRA)
1984	I Lendl (TCH)
1985	M Wilander (SWE)
1986	I Lendl (TCH)
1987	I Lendl (TCH)
1988	M Wilander (SWE)
1989	M Chang (USA)
1990	A Gomez (ECU)
1991	J Courier (USA)
1992	J Courier (USA)
1993	S Bruguera (ESP)

Women's Singles	
1979	C Evert-Lloyd (USA)
1980	C Evert-Lloyd (USA)
1981	H Mandlikova (TCH)
1982	M Navratilova (USA)
1983	C Evert-Lloyd (USA)
1984	M Navratilova (USA)
1985	C Evert-Lloyd (USA)
1986	C Evert-Lloyd (USA)
1987	S Graf (FRG)
1988	S Graf (FRG)
1989	A Sanchez (ESP)
1990	M Seles (YUG)
1991	M Seles (YUG)
1992	M Seles (YUG)
1993	S Graf (GER)

Men's Singles *cont.*
1994 S Bruguera (ESP)
1995 T Muster (AUT)
1996 Y Kafelnikov (RUS)
1997 G Kuerten (BRA)
1998 C Moya (ESP)
1999 A Agassi (USA)
2000 G Kuerten (BRA)
2001 G Kuerten (BRA)
2002 A Costa (ESP)
2003 J C Ferrero (ESP)
2004 G Gaudio (ARG)

Women's Singles *cont.*
1994 A Sanchez-Vicario (ESP)
1995 S Graf (GER)
1996 S Graf (GER)
1997 I Majoli (CRO)
1998 A Sanchez-Vicario (ESP)
1999 S Graf (GER)
2000 M Pierce (FRA)
2001 J Capriati (USA)
2002 S Williams (USA)
2003 J Henin-Hardenne (BEL)
2004 A Myskina (RUS)

US Open Championships

The last Grand Slam event of the year is traditionally staged at Flushing Meadows, New York. The Men's Singles was first won by R D Sears in 1881 and the Women's Singles by E Hansell in 1887. Previous winners from 1979.

Men's Singles
1979 J P McEnroe (USA)
1980 J P McEnroe (USA)
1981 J P McEnroe (USA)
1982 J Connors (USA)
1983 J Connors (USA)
1984 J P McEnroe (USA)
1985 I Lendl (TCH)
1986 I Lendl (TCH)

Women's Singles
1979 T Austin (USA)
1980 C Evert-Lloyd (USA)
1981 T Austin (USA)
1982 C Evert-Lloyd (USA)
1983 M Navratilova (USA)
1984 M Navratilova (USA)
1985 H Mandlikova (TCH)
1986 M Navratilova (USA)

Men's Singles *cont.*

1987 I Lendl (TCH)
1988 M Wilander (SWE)
1989 B Becker (GER)
1990 P Sampras (USA)
1991 S Edberg (SWE)
1992 S Edberg (SWE)
1993 P Sampras (USA)
1994 A Agassi (USA)
1995 P Sampras (USA)
1996 P Sampras (USA)
1997 P Rafter (AUS)
1998 P Rafter (AUS)
1999 A Agassi (USA)
2000 M Safin (RUS)
2001 L Hewitt (AUS)
2002 P Sampras (USA)
2003 A Roddick (USA)
2004 R Federer (SUI)

Women's Singles *cont.*

1987 M Navratilova (USA)
1988 S Graf (FRG)
1989 S Graf (FRG)
1990 G Sabatini (ARG)
1991 M Seles (YUG)
1992 M Seles (YUG)
1993 S Graf (GER)
1994 A Sanchez-Vicario (ESP)
1995 S Graf (GER)
1996 S Graf (GER)
1997 M Hingis (SUI)
1998 L Davenport (USA)
1999 S Williams (USA)
2000 V Williams (USA)
2001 V Williams (USA)
2002 S Williams (USA)
2003 J Henin-Hardenne (BEL)
2004 S Kuznetsova (RUS)

General Interest

INTERNATIONAL TIME ZONES

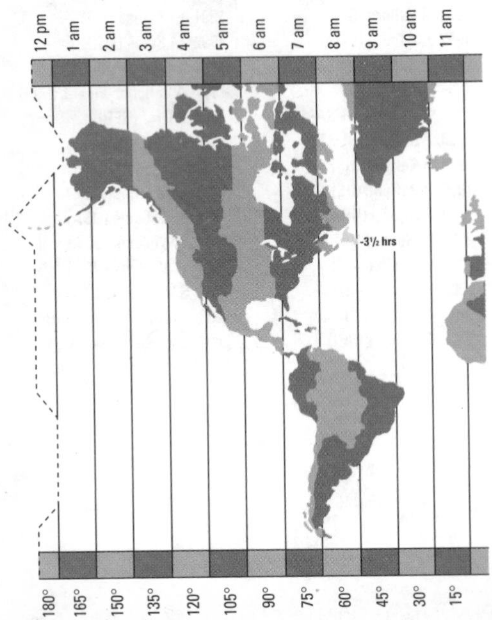

The system was established in 1884 by agreement between the major countries. The meridian of longitude passing through Greenwich Observatory, London, was taken as the starting-point for 24 time zones (each, generally, representing 15° of longitude,

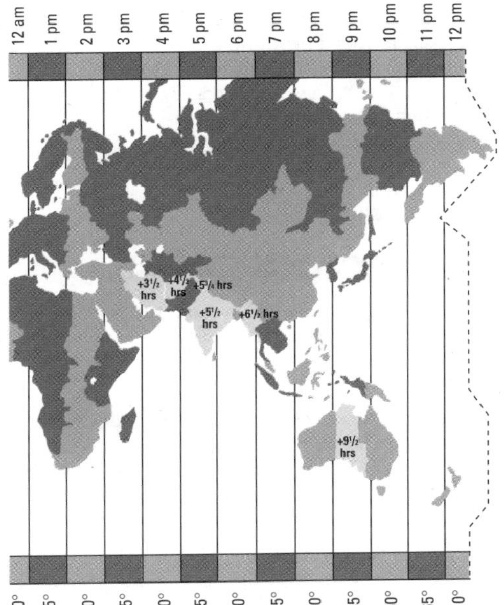

the equivalent of 1 hour). There are 12 time zones west of Greenwich and 12 east. Within a time zone the time is the same throughout, but when crossing from one zone to another, the time changes by 1 hour. The world is divided into 23 full zones and 2 half zones, zone 12 east and zone 12 west, which are adjacent and separated by an imaginary line, the International Date Line, halfway round the world from Greenwich. Thus a traveller crossing the line and heading west will lose a day, and if heading east will gain a day. See also **The International Date Line**.

Note: Several countries, including the UK, use Daylight Saving Time (DST) in order to maximize daylight time in summer. Clocks are put forward 1 hour in spring and back 1 hour in autumn. The plan on pages 290–1 does not take account of DST adjustments.

THE INTERNATIONAL DATE LINE

This is an imaginary line which marks the place on the earth's surface where each new calendar day begins. The date on the west of the date line is one day later than on the east.

The International Date Line follows the 180th meridian for most of its length but is adjusted where necessary to avoid having two different calendar dates on the same day in a fairly small country. The 180th meridian is exactly halfway round the world from Greenwich, London.

The sun travels over 15° of the earth's surface each

hour. For each 15° west of Greenwich, the time reverses one hour. At longitude 180° east the time is 12 hours ahead of Greenwich time. At longitude 180° west, the time is 12 hours behind Greenwich. Thus there is a 24-hour time difference between the two sides of the 180th meridian.

A new date begins first on the western side of the date line. As the earth rotates on its axis, this new date sweeps westwards over the earth and the date covers the entire earth in 24 hours. See also **International Time Zones**.

CALENDARS

There are three main types of calendar:

Lunar Calendar

Most ancient calendars used the interval between successive full moons, the lunar month, as a measure of time. The lunar month is approximately 29½ days in length; thus a lunar year (12 x 29½) amounts to approximately 354 days. This means that its year is approximately 11 days shorter than the true solar year (approximately 365 days), and following it would cause the seasons to occur earlier and earlier each year. This makes the lunar calendar alone unsuitable for practical use.

Solar Calendar

The solar calendar adheres as closely as possible to the length of the solar year, but assumes a set length of month, thereby disregarding the lunar month. The solar year is 365.2422 days in length. Solar calendars use a normal year of 365 days and allow for the fraction (0.2422 days) by inserting an extra day every fourth year. The solar calendar has 4 critical points: 2 equinoxes and 2 solstices (see page 302). The fact that the equinoxes always occur on or about the same days each year establishes the accuracy of such a calendar.

Lunisolar Calendar

The lunisolar calendar is an attempt to reconcile the differences between the lunar and solar calendars. The lunar month of 29½ days becomes either a 29- or 30-day month (alternately), thus making 354 days. Additional months are inserted from time to time to adjust the number of calendar days to the number of days in a solar year. This is usually done by inserting a 13th lunar month every 2 or 3 years, thus ensuring that the seasons accord approximately with the calendar period.

CALENDARS IN USE TODAY

Gregorian Calendar

The Gregorian calendar is used almost universally throughout the western world, and has been used in Great Britain since 1752. It was calculated by Pope Gregory XIII in the 1580s in an attempt to reform the Roman Julian calendar which had become inaccurate and confusing. As the true length of the solar year was then known, Gregory simplified and adapted the Julian calendar accordingly.

The Gregorian calendar has 12 months, 11 with either 30 or 31 days; February has 28 days and, every fourth year (a leap year), 29 days. However, these adjustments are still not quite enough to ensure absolute accuracy and so in century years that cannot be divided by 400 (1700, 1800, 1900), February loses its leap year. The Gregorian calendar is so accurate that the difference between calendar and solar years is approximately 26 seconds. This difference will increase by 0.53 second each century because the solar year is gradually becoming shorter. The western calendar is based on the year of Jesus Christ's birth; dates before this event are noted BC (Before Christ), and those after as AD (Anno Domini, In the Year of our Lord). Non-Christians often prefer BCE (Before Christian Era) and CE (Christian Era).

Month	Derived from	Length (days)
January	*Januarius* (Latin). The Roman god, Janus, faces two ways and was often represented on doorways and archways.	31
February	*Februarius* (Latin). Taken from Februa, a purification rite which took place on February 15.	28 or 29
March	*Martius* (Latin). Mars was the Roman god of war.	31
April	*Aprilis* (Latin). Taken from *aperire* ('to open'), referring to the trees and flowers which are beginning to open.	30
May	*Maius* (Latin). Derived either from Maia, a Roman goddess identified with the Greek goddess Maia, or from *maiores* ('elders'), referring to the period in which old people were honoured.	31

Month	Derived from	Length (days)
June	*Junius* (Latin). Derived either from the goddess Juno or *iuniores* ('young people'), indicating the period which was traditionally dedicated to young people.	30
July	*Julius* (Latin). Named after Gaius Julius Caesar, the Roman soldier and statesman.	31
August	*Augustus* (Latin). Named after Augustus Caesar, the first Roman Emperor.	31
September	*Septem* (Latin), meaning 'seven'; September was originally the seventh month in the Roman calendar.	30
October	*Octo* (Latin), meaning 'eight'; October was originally the eighth month in the Roman calendar.	31
November	*Novem* (Latin), meaning 'nine'; November was originally the ninth month in the Roman calendar.	30
December	*Decem* (Latin), meaning 'ten'; December was originally the tenth month in the Roman calendar.	31

The Christian Church Calendar is governed partly by the sun and partly by the moon. The dates of fixed feasts such as Christmas and saints' days relate to the solar calendar, whereas the date of Easter – and therefore of all the movable feasts and holy days – is determined by the date of the Paschal Full Moon.

Jewish Calendar

The Jewish calendar was begun, traditionally, at the moment of creation, 3760 years and 3 months before the beginning of the Christian era. To find the Jewish year, add 3760 years to the date in the Gregorian calendar. Thus, the Gregorian year 2003 will be 5763 in the Jewish calendar. As a lunisolar calendar, the Jewish calendar requires an extra month (Veadar) to be inserted seven times in a 19-year cycle; Veadar is inserted between Adar and Nisan and Adar is given 30 days instead of 29.

Month	**Length (days)**
Nisan	(March/April in Gregorian calendar) 30
Iyar	29
Sivan	30
Tammuz	29
Ab	30
Elul	29
Tishri	30
Heshvan	29/30
Kislev	29/30
Tebet	29
Shebat	30
Adar	29/30

Note: Nisan is the first month of the Jewish year, although years are numbered from Tishri, the seventh month.

Islamic Calendar

The Islamic calendar begins with Muhammad's flight from Mecca to Medina (the Hegira) in AD 622. As a lunar calendar the year is much shorter than the solar year and, as no adjustments are made, it moves fully backwards through the seasons over a period of 32½ years. Time is divided into 30-year cycles; during each cycle 19 years have the usual 354 days and 11 years take an extra day each. The Islamic year is based on the moon and has 12 months, alternately of 30 and 29 days.

Month	Length (days)
Muharram	30
Safar	29
Rabi I	30
Rabi II	29
Jumada I	30
Jumada II	29
Rajab	30
Shaban	29
Ramadan	30
Shawwal	29
Zulkadah	30
Zulhijjah	29*

* *Takes an extra day in leap years*

Hindu Calendar

The Hindu calendar dates from about 1000 BC and was first used in India. It is a lunar calendar, so an additional month (Adhik) is incorporated every 30 months to remove the discrepancy between the lunar year (approximately 354 days) and the solar year (approximately 365 days). There are 12 months of 30 days each, divided into Shukla (the light fortnight) and Krishna (the dark fortnight).

Hindu Month Names

Chait'r (March/April in Gregorian calendar)
Vaishaakh
Jayshyth
Aashaadh
Shraawan
Bhaadrap'd
Aashwin
Kaartik
Maargasheersh
Paush
Maagh
Phaalgun

Chinese Calendar

The Chinese calendar began in 2637 BC when Emperor Huangdi is said to have invented it. It is a lunar calendar and years are calculated in cycles of 60 (e.g. 2003 is the 20th year in the 78th cycle).

There is a Buddhist belief that the Buddha invited all the animals to celebrate the New Year with him but only 12 came. As a reward the Buddha named a year after each of them in the order in which they arrived in his presence, with the rat first and the pig last.

The Chinese year is based on the moon and has 12 months, each beginning at a new moon with 29 or 30 days. A month is repeated seven times during each 19-year cycle so that the calendar stays approximately in line with the seasons. The Chinese New Year occurs at the second new moon after the beginning of winter; thus it is no earlier than 20 January and no later than 20 February.

Note: The official Chinese calendar now corresponds with the western system, but the old calendar is still used in Tibet, Hong Kong, Singapore, Malaysia and other parts of south-east Asia.

Animal	Year							
Rat	1900	1912	1924	1936	1948	1960	1972	1984	1996
Buffalo or Cow	1901	1913	1925	1937	1949	1961	1973	1985	1997
Tiger	1902	1914	1926	1938	1950	1962	1974	1986	1998
Rabbit	1903	1915	1927	1939	1951	1963	1975	1987	1999
Dragon	1904	1916	1928	1940	1952	1964	1976	1988	2000
Snake	1905	1917	1929	1941	1953	1965	1977	1989	2001
Horse	1906*	1918	1930	1942	1954	1966*	1978	1990	2002
Goat	1907	1919	1931	1943	1955	1967	1979	1991	2003
Monkey	1908	1920	1932	1944	1956	1968	1980	1992	2004
Rooster or Chicken	1909	1921	1933	1945	1957	1969	1981	1993	2005
Dog	1910	1922	1934	1946	1958	1970	1982	1994	2006
Pig	1911	1923	1935	1947	1959	1971	1983	1995	2007

** Called Fire Horse once every 60 years*

FRENCH REVOLUTIONARY CALENDAR

The French Revolutionary Calendar was an attempt by the First French Republic to reform the Gregorian calendar in line with revolutionary principles. It was adopted in 1793 and abandoned in 1805.

Vendémiaire (Month of Grape Harvest)	23 September–22 October
Brumaire (Month of Mist)	23 October–21 November
Frimaire (Frosty Month)	22 November–21 December
Nivôse (Snowy Month)	22 December–20 January
Pluviôse (Rainy Month)	21 January–19 February
Ventôse (Windy Month)	20 February–21 March
Germinal (Month of Buds)	22 March–20 April
Floréal (Month of Flowers)	21 April–20 May
Prairial (Month of Meadows)	21 May–19 June
Messidor (Month of Harvest)	20 June–19 July
Thermidor (Month of Heat)	20 July–18 August
Fructidor (Month of Fruit)	19 August–22 September

SOLSTICE

The time when the sun is farthest from the equator and appears to stand still. Occurs twice yearly. In the Northern Hemisphere:

Winter Solstice (around 22 December) = shortest day
Summer Solstice (around 21 June) = longest day

EQUINOX

The time when the sun crosses the equator and day and night are equal. Occurs twice yearly. In the Northern Hemisphere:

Spring (Vernal) Equinox (around 21 March)
Autumnal Equinox (around 23 September)

QUARTER DAYS (ENGLAND, WALES AND NORTHERN IRELAND)

The four days of the year when certain payments become due.

Lady Day	25 March
Midsummer	24 June
Michaelmas	29 September
Christmas	25 December

SCOTTISH TERM DAYS

A division of the academic year when schools, colleges or universities are in session, and one of the periods of time during which sessions of courts of law are held.

Candlemas 2 February	Feast of the Purification of the Virgin Mary and the day on which church candles are blessed.
Whit Sunday 7th Sunday after Easter	Commemorates the descent of the Holy Spirit after Easter (movable) on the day of Pentecost. Whit (or white) Sunday was so called because white robes were worn on that day.
Lammas 1 August	Feast commemorating St Peter's miraculous delivery from prison. Formerly observed in England as a Harvest Festival, when loaves made from the first ripe corn were consecrated. (Origin: Old English *hlafmaesse*, 'loaf mass'.)
Martinmas 11 November	Feast of St Martin, formerly day for hiring servants and slaughtering cattle to be salted for the winter.

BIRTHSTONES, ASTROLOGICAL SIGNS AND NAMES

Month	Gem	Characteristic
January	Garnet	Constancy
February	Amethyst	Sincerity
March	Aquamarine, Bloodstone	Courage
April	Diamond	Innocence
May	Emerald	Love
June	Pearl, Alexandrite, Moonstone	Health
July	Ruby	Contentment
August	Peridot, Sardonyx	Married happiness
September	Sapphire	Clear thinking
October	Opal, Tourmaline	Hope
November	Topaz	Faithfulness
December	Turquoise, Zircon	Wealth

305

Corresponding Astrological (Zodiac) Sign*
♒ Aquarius (20 January–18 February)
♓ Pisces (19 February–20 March)
♈ Aries (21 March–19 April)
♉ Taurus (20 April–20 May)
♊ Gemini (21 May–20 June)
♋ Cancer (21 June–22 July)
♌ Leo (23 July–22 August)
♍ Virgo (23 August–22 September)
♎ Libra (23 September–22 October)
♏ Scorpio (23 October–21 November)
♐ Sagittarius (22 November–21 December)
♑ Capricorn (22 December–19 January)

** Astrological signs do not correspond exactly with the beginning and end of the month; birthdate should be the guide to the appropriate gemstone*

WEDDING ANNIVERSARIES

Year	Gift
1	Paper, plastics, furniture
2	Cotton, china
3	Leather or artificial leather articles
4	Linen, silk or synthetic silks
5	Wood and decorative articles for the home
6	Iron
7	Wood, copper, brass
8	Bronze, electrical appliances
9	Pottery, china, glass, crystal
10	Tin, aluminium
11	Steel
12	Linen, silk, nylon
13	Lace
14	Ivory, agate
15	Crystal, glass
20	China, small items of furniture
25	Silver
30	Pearls or personal gifts
35	Coral, jade
40	Rubies, garnets
45	Sapphires, tourmalines
50	Gold
55	Emeralds, turquoises
60, 75	Diamonds, gold

ORDERS OF PRECEDENCE

The Peerage

Title Royal Duke/Duchess
Style His Royal Highness the Duke of . . . /
Her Royal Highness the Duchess of . . .
Addressed as Sir or, formally, May it please your Royal Highness

Title Archbishop
Style The Most Reverend His Grace the Lord Archbishop of . . .
Addressed as My Lord Archbishop or Your Grace

Title Duke/Duchess
Style His Grace the Duke of . . . /
Her Grace the Duchess of . . .
Addressed as My Lord Duke/
Your Grace; Dear Madam/Duchess*

Title Marquess/Marchioness
Style The Most Honourable the Marquess of . . . /
The Most Honourable the Marchioness of . . .
Addressed as My Lord/My Lord; Madam/Lady*

Title Earl/Countess
Style The Right Honourable The Earl of . . . /
The Right Honourable the Countess of . . .
Addressed as My Lord/My Lord; Madam/Madam*

Title Viscount/Viscountess
Style The Right Honourable the Viscount . . . /
The Right Honourable the Viscountess . . .
Addressed as My Lord/My Lord; Madam/Lady*

Title Bishop
Style The Right Reverend the Lord Bishop of . . .
Addressed as My Lord

Title Baron/Baroness
Style The Right Honourable the Lord . . . /
The Right Honourable the Lady . . .
Addressed as My Lord/Lord; My Lady/Lady*

** This section shows the correct forms of address for letters (formal) and when speaking (formal)*

PRINCIPAL BRITISH ORDERS AND DECORATIONS IN ORDER OF PRECEDENCE

Title	Date of Institution	Abbreviation
Knight of the Garter	1348	KG
Knight of the Thistle	809	KT
Knight of St Patrick	1783*	KP
Knight Grand Cross of the Bath	1725	GCB
Order of Merit	1902	OM
Knight Grand Commander, Star of India	1861	GCSI
Knight Grand Cross, St Michael and St George	1818	GCMG

Title	Date of Institution	Abbreviation
Knight Grand Commander, Order of the Indian Empire	1878*	GCIE
Crown of India (Ladies)	1878*	CI
Knight Grand Cross, Victorian Order	1896	GCVO
Knight Grand Cross, British Empire	1917	GBE
Companions of Honour	1917	CH
Knight Commander, Bath	1725	KCB
Knight Commander, Star of India	1861	KCSI
Knight Commander, St Michael and St George	1818	KCMG
Knight Commander, Indian Empire	1878*	KCIE
Knight Commander, Victorian Order	1896	KCVO
Knight Commander, British Empire	1917	KBE
Knights Bachelor	**	Kt
Companion, Bath	1725	CB
Companion, Star of India	1861	CSI
Companion, St Michael and St George	1818	CMG
Companion, Indian Empire	1878*	CIE
Commander, Victorian Order	1896	CVO
Commander, British Empire	1917	CBE
Companion, Distinguished Service Order	1886	DSO
Order of the British Empire	1917	OBE
Companion, Imperial Service Order	1902	ISO
Member, British Empire	1917	MBE
Indian Order of Merit	1837*	IOM
Order of British India	1837*	OBI

** Obsolete ** Not an order; entitles the recipient to be called 'Sir' but knighthood cannot be passed on to heirs. Awarded for distinguished service*

DECORATIONS FOR GALLANTRY AND DISTINGUISHED SERVICE

Title	Date of Institution	Abbreviation
Victoria Cross	1856	VC
George Cross	1940	GC
Conspicuous Gallantry Cross	1995	CGC
Distinguished Service Order	1886	DSO
Distinguished Service Cross	1901	DSC
Military Cross	1914	MC
Distinguished Flying Cross	1918	DFC
Air Force Cross	1918	AFC
Albert Medal	1866	AM
Distinguished Conduct Medal (army)	1845	DCM
Conspicuous Gallantry Medal (navy & RAF)	1855, 1874	CGM
George Medal	1940	GM
Distinguished Service Medal (navy)	1914	DSM
Military Medal	1916	MM
Distinguished Flying Medal	1918	DFM
British Empire Medal	1917*	BEM

THE ARMED FORCES

The Army

Field Marshal

General (Gen)

Lieutenant-General (Lt-Gen)

Major-General (Maj-Gen)

Brigadier (Brig)

Colonel (Col)

Lieutenant-Colonel (Lt-Col)

Major (Maj)

Captain (Capt)

Lieutenant (Lt)

Second Lieutenant (2nd Lt)

Warrant Officer
Staff Sergeant
Sergeant
Corporal
Lance Corporal
Private

The Royal Navy

Admiral of the Fleet

Admiral (Adm)

Vice-Admiral (Vice-Adm)

Rear-Admiral (Rear-Adm)

Commodore (1st and 2nd Class) (Cdre)

Captain (Capt)

Commander (Cdr)

Lieutenant-Commander (Lt-Cdr)

Lieutenant (Lt)

Sub-Lieutenant (Sub-Lt)

Midshipman
(Displayed on lapel)

Fleet Chief Petty Officer
Chief Petty Officer
Petty Officer
Leading Rating (or Seaman)
Able Rating (or Seaman)
Junior Rating (or Seaman)

The Royal Air Force

Marshal of the RAF

Air Chief Marshal

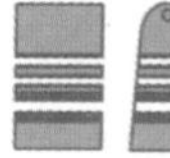

Air Marshal

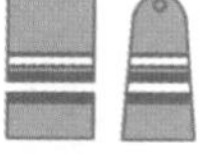

Air Vice-Marshal

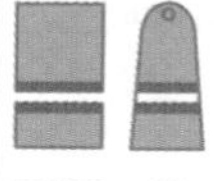

Air Commodore (Air Cdre)

Group Captain (Gp Capt)

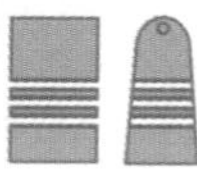

Wing Commander (Wg Cdr)

Squadron Leader (Squ Ldr)

Flight Lieutenant (Flt Lt)

Flying Officer (FO)

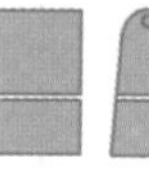

Pilot Officer (PO)

Acting Pilot Officer
Warrant Officer
Flight Sergeant
Sergeant
Corporal
Junior Technician
Senior Aircraftman
Leading Aircraftman
Aircraftman

THE POLICE

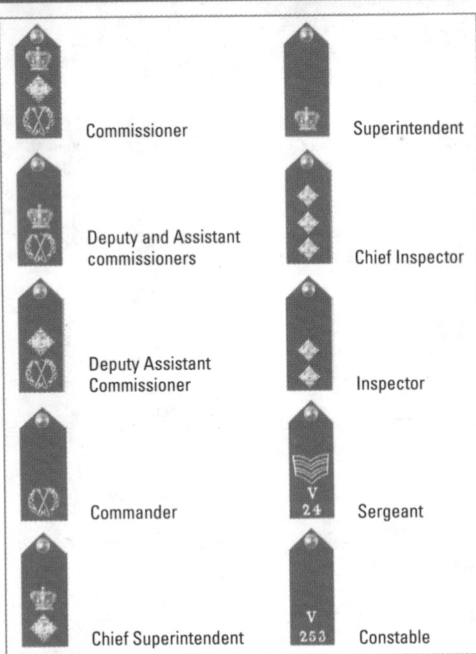

Published by courtesy of the Metropolitan Police Service.

THE KNIGHTS OF THE ROUND TABLE

King Arthur's knights were so-called because of the large, circular table around which they sat and which gave precedence to none, save the king. Popularly thought to have numbered 12, some sources indicate there were many more, even as many as 150. The following list gives the names of the best known.

Sir Kay	Sir Bedivere
Sir Gareth	Sir Gawain
Sir Lancelot du Lac	Sir Tristan de Lyonnais
Sir Galahad	Sir Perceval
Sir Bors	Sir Ector
Sir Tarquin	Sir Lionel
Sir Mordred*	

* *Mordred was Arthur's son and ultimately responsible for his downfall*

THE FOUR TEMPERAMENTS OR HUMOURS

These were thought to represent the dominant characteristics of human beings, an idea first put forward by Aristotle. It was recognized that individuals are a mixture of all four traits, but the theory held that every person showed one of the four temperaments as a ruling quality. The humours are the four principal bodily fluids and each of the temperaments is characterized by the prevailing influence of one of the humours.

Temperament	Humour	Character
Sanguine	Blood	Cheerfulness
Melancholic	Black bile	Gloominess
Choleric	Yellow bile	Anger
Lethargic or phlegmatic	Phlegm	Apathy

THE SEVEN LIBERAL ARTS

This classification dates from the Middle Ages and was taken to be the basis of secular education.

The Trivium – Logic, Grammar, Rhetoric
The Quadrivium – Arithmetic, Geometry, Astronomy, Music

THE SIX WIVES OF HENRY VIII

1. Catherine of Aragon (divorced)
2. Anne Boleyn (beheaded)
3. Jane Seymour (died)
4. Anne of Cleves (divorced)
5. Catherine Howard (beheaded)
6. Catherine Parr (survived)

THE THREE GRACES (GREEK MYTHOLOGY)

Three sister goddesses, givers of charm and beauty.

Aglaia
Euphrosyne
Thalia; one of the Nine Muses

THE NINE MUSES (GREEK MYTHOLOGY)

Nine sister goddesses, daughters of Zeus and Mnemosyne, each regarded as protectress of a different art or science.

Name	Muse of
Calliope	Epic Poetry
Clio	History
Erato	Love Poetry
Euterpe	Lyric Poetry and Music
Melpomene	Tragedy
Polyhymnia	Singing, Mime and Sacred Dance
Terpsichore	Dance and Choral Song
Thalia	Comedy and Pastoral Poetry; one of the Three Graces
Urania	Astronomy

THE LABOURS OF HERCULES

To slay the Nemean lion and bring back its skin
To kill the Lernean Hydra
To catch and retain the Arcadian stag (Ceryneian hind)
To destroy the Erymanthean boar
To cleanse the stables of King Augeas, King of Elis
To destroy the cannibal birds of Lake Stymphalis
To capture the Cretan bull
To catch the horses of the Thracian Diomedes who fed them on human flesh

The Labours of Hercules *cont.*

To get possession of the girdle of Hippolyte, Queen of the Amazons, and bring it to Admete, daughter of Eurystheus
To capture the oxen of the monster Geryon
To get possession of the apples of the Hesperides
To bring up from the infernal regions the three-headed dog, Cerberus

THE SEVEN VIRTUES

Faith, Hope and Charity are called the Holy Virtues.

Faith	Prudence	Fortitude	Hope
Justice	Temperance	Charity	

THE SEVEN WONDERS OF THE ANCIENT WORLD

Pyramids of Egypt
Hanging Gardens of Babylon
Statue of Zeus at Olympia
Temple of Artemis at Ephesus
Mausoleum of Halicarnassus
Colossus of Rhodes
Pharos (lighthouse) of Alexandria

THE SEVEN SEAS

North Pacific Ocean
South Pacific Ocean
North Atlantic Ocean
South Atlantic Ocean
Arctic Ocean
Antarctic Ocean
Indian Ocean

THE SEVEN DEADLY SINS

Pride
Gluttony
Covetousness
Anger
Lust
Sloth
Envy

THE TWELVE DAYS OF CHRISTMAS

Traditional English carol.

My true love sent to me
A partridge in a pear tree,
Two turtle doves,
Three French hens,
Four calling birds,
Five gold rings,
Six geese a-laying,
Seven swans a-swimming,
Eight maids a-milking,
Nine ladies dancing,
Ten lords a-leaping,
Eleven pipers piping,
Twelve drummers drumming.

THE MAGNIFICENT SEVEN

Listed below are the names of the actors who played the eponymous seven gunfighters in the famous 1960 Western movie directed by John Sturges.

Charles Bronson	Brad Dexter
Yul Brynner	Steve McQueen
Horst Buchholz	Robert Vaughn
James Coburn	

THE SEVEN DWARFS

Listed below are the names of the seven dwarfs appearing in Walt Disney's full-length cartoon feature *Snow White and the Seven Dwarfs* (1937).

Bashful	Dopey	Happy	Sneezy
Doc	Grumpy	Sleepy	

THE THREE MUSKETEERS

The names of the eponymous heroes of the novel by Alexandre Dumas (1844).

Aramis Athos Porthos

The name of their comrade, the 'fourth musketeer', is:

D'Artagnan